HEALING

Understanding
HEALING

KURT W. WALLACE

TATE PUBLISHING
AND **ENTERPRISES**, LLC

Published by Tate Publishing & Enterprises, LLC
127 E. Trade Center Terrace | Mustang, Oklahoma 73064 USA
1.888.361.9473 | www.tatepublishing.com

Tate Publishing is committed to excellence in the publishing industry. The company reflects the philosophy established by the founders, based on Psalm 68:11,
"The Lord gave the word and great was the company of those who published it."

Book design copyright © 2014 by Tate Publishing, LLC. All rights reserved.
Cover design by Carlo Nino Suico
Interior design by Mary Jean Archival

Published in the United States of America

ISBN: 978-1-63306-443-0
Religion / Christian Life / Inspirational
14.09.04

Dedication

I want to dedicate this book to some very special people who continually impact my life on a daily basis. First, let me give a shout out to three sisters. First, Maureen Blackburn and Tiffany Brown who helped me in writing this book. Both of these ladies operate in a spirit-filled anointed healing ministry and are full of faith. Their insights and passion for the key themes to address, I believe, has made this book richer. To Dianne Ryder, my editor, thank you so much for putting up with me and all my quirks. I cannot express my appreciation for your tireless work on this project. I am going to miss those working dinners at Thai Orchid.

Then there are those who gave the book meaning and depth with your testimonies. Your genuine life encounters give evidence to God's love and care for his people. Continue to give God glory and tell of his goodness.

And to my wife, Suzanne, there are not enough words to express my love for you. Your strength in the Lord continues to show. We never knew how important this book would be to us. I thank God that you continue to stand with me and keep me true to God's calling on my life and ours together.

And I am most humbled and grateful for my God, my Lord and Savior Jesus Christ, and the Holy Spirit, my friend. I found that although I have been walking with the Lord for more than twenty-nine years, being a seminary graduate, serving on church staffs, being a church planter, and counseling countless people (and the list goes on), I must say I have never learned to lean on the Lord and trust him as I am doing now. Thank you for making the journey of writing this book real to me. God, Jesus, and Holy Spirit, I love you so much.

Contents

Introduction

"I am the resurrection and the life. He who believes in Me, though he may die, he shall live. And whoever lives and believes in Me shall never die. Do you believe this?"

John 11:25-26 (NKJV)

U*nderstanding Healing* is a book to help followers of Christ to know how to exercise their faith in prayer as they walk in the steps of Jesus on this side of heaven, as well as look forward to eternal life with much hope. In many church circles and denominations today, there are many false manifestations of healing. But just the same, there are many places where the presence and power of God is manifested in ways that result in national, physical, and spiritual healing. I am appalled by those in Christian circles today who are attacking Charismatic believers because we believe in the present ministry of the Holy Spirit through spiritual gifts, signs, and wonders.

One of the first spoken words the Holy Spirit pressed on my heart as a young believer was simply "more." More of what? you ask. Simply "more" of God. I knew I served the God of the universe, the Creator, the One who does what he wants according to his will, and that I was his child. As a growing believer, I knew and still believe that God can and does perform signs and wonders in the earth, and he still works and demonstrates his power through his people.

For the Charismatic church, let's make it our aim to do all that we do to be well pleasing to the Lord. Let's continue to walk in the Spirit as he works, and then, let's join him in his work. The good news is that he is always at work. Let's seek his face and yield to him. Don't get ahead of him producing false manifestations of spiritual gifts. *Understanding Healing* is by no means the final authority on this topic, but I do pray that it will help you discern how to pray and walk with God by knowing how he is working and then, by faith, join him in his work. I am trusting God each day for my healing, and I know that when he is finished, I shall be like him.

Understanding Healing

The topic or, should I say, the doctrine of healing can be confusing at times. It is, however, a doctrine that needs to be understood. Oftentimes, it is misunderstood as to how it happens, why it happens, and who receives it. As I understand the Scriptures, there are a few things we need to understand about healing. First and foremost, God wants everything he created in perfect unity with him. Since the fall of humanity, God's goal has been to redeem humanity back to himself. In the Old Testament, we see this process given through the law, and although the law was imperfect, it did lead us to God's Son, Jesus Christ, who redeemed us from the curse of the law.[1] When a person is redeemed, a renewal occurs within—this is when healing begins. The need for healing is universal; we are in desperate need for spiritual, physical, and national healing.

National healing: Our nation is similar to the people of God in the book of Judges, chapters 17 and 21 where it is recorded that, "everyone did what was right in their own eyes." This need for healing came as a result of the people of God turning away from God's moral as well as ethical standards. Each of the families became self-reliant. They only cared about their own stuff, which caused them to take their eyes off the Lord. Sadly, they forgot about all that God had done to protect and care for them. They forgot all his promises and how he delivered them from the hand of Pharaoh and led them through the wilderness.

Physical healing takes place in many different ways, as God directs. We will find that it can come over a period of time, in this lifetime, or when a person enters eternity. Healing can also happen immediately without the aid of medicines or a doctor's care. Lastly, as mentioned, a person may need a doctor's care, and may be prescribed medicine to aid in the care and healing process.

Spiritual healing is the most important of the three. The centerpiece of spiritual healing is the gospel of

Jesus Christ. The Scriptures reveal to us that there is no remission for sin without his sacrificial death on the cross to redeem us from the penalty of sin.[2] The good news is that Jesus didn't come to die for some, but for all. Those who trust and believe that Jesus Christ is the Son of God and that he gave his life for us as atonement for sin will be healed from the curse of eternal separation from the presence of God and inherit eternal life.

Whether the need for healing is national, physical, or spiritual, the answer is the same. We need to turn to God, for he is the remedy for the sin that afflicts us all.[3] Healing requires an extraordinary faith and longsuffering as we look to God and wait for it even as we pursue it.

I believe everyone in the body of Christ has an anointed God-given opportunity to operate and participate in God's healing ministry. God is calling each of us into a deeper personal relationship with him through his Son, Jesus Christ. This is a time to surrender and trust God to lead us, guide us, and take care of us— yes, to put him first in all areas of our lives. You see, God has a purpose for our lives. Even more so, our purpose is connected to his kingdom's purposes that all would know him and turn back our wayward hearts. This poses a challenge for some, but it is worth it all. In order to tap into this area of your purpose, you must have faith.

> But without faith it is impossible to please Him,
> for he who comes to God must believe that He is,
> and that He is a rewarder of those who diligently
> seek Him.

Hebrews 11:6 (NKJV)

I pray that my study and understanding of the Scriptures are accurate and lead us into a Spirit-filled healing culture in our personal lives and within our ecclesiastical community. I pray for those who have the gift of healing to have a greater discernment of how God is moving in the life of the believer and in the midst of Jesus's church. I also believe that with healing, there is a partnering gift of prophecy as well as the gift of performing miracles. There are other gifts that support this mix (faith, wisdom, and discernment), but I believe these two are eminent.

Prophecy is the special ability that God gives to certain members of the body of Christ to receive and communicate an immediate message of God to his people through a divinely anointed utterance (Luke 7:26; Acts 15:32; Acts 2:19; Romans 12:6; 1 Corinthians 12:10, 28; and Ephesians 4:11–13). (Reference: *Your Spiritual Gifts*, Peter Wagner)

Performing miracles is the special ability that God gives to certain members of the body of Christ to serve as human intermediaries through whom it pleases God to perform powerful acts that are perceived by observers to have altered the ordinary course of nature (Acts 9:36–42; Acts 19:11–20; Acts 20:7–12; Romans 15:18–19; 1 Corinthians 12:10, 28; 2 Corinthians 12:12).

These gifts are somewhat inseparable in their dispensation. I would also suggest that if you suffer from lack of compassion toward others, then you would probably be challenged with this ministry. Compassion is to care for and have sympathy for others who are struggling to the point where you are compelled to do something about it. Let me encourage you to pray and ask God to give you his heart for the health and well being of his children. God's motivation to heal is love, and because he loves, he acts.

The word "heal" or "healing," in Scripture is conveyed alongside other terms such as, "cure" and "whole." These two terms communicate a different piece to understanding how God chooses to heal. The word "heal" is used in the verb form because it is an action performed by another. As we pursue the understanding of healing, we must first understand that God is the source for our healing.

God Is the Divine Source

In the Old Testament, we see that God is our healer. The Hebrew name is "Jehovah *Rāpā*," "Jehovah *Raphe*," or "Jehovah *Rophe*," meaning that the existing one God is able to restore and to make healthy—"*to heal*." The form of this word meaning "to heal" is used more than sixty-five times in the Old Testament. The first usage is found in Genesis 20:17, where we find Abraham praying for Abimelech, the king of Gerar. Abraham and his family journeyed from Canaan toward Gerar. Abraham was in strange territory, and so he was afraid of King Abimelech. He thought that King Abimelech was going to kill him and take his wife for himself, so he lied, enlisting Sarah's consent. Their plot was to say that Sarah was Abraham's sister. While King Abimelech was sleeping, God spoke to him in a dream and told him he was a dead man if he touched Sarah in any way. This, by the way, would have been adultery. "So Abraham prayed to God; and God healed Abimelech" (Genesis 20:17, NKJV).

God is the ultimate divine healer. He is able to restore to normal any physical or spiritual abnormality within his people and his land according to his nature and his covenant toward his people. In fact, we hallow (sanctify, bless, respect) God when we choose to serve him—when we put him first above all else. We need to be restored to a healthy relationship with God, and this is accomplished when we choose to repent. Repentance is genuine when it results in turning our hearts to God (Psalm 6:2, Jeremiah 17:14, and Psalm 107:20). You see, God always heals, but in different ways in respect to the now and eternity. In other words, healing can happen over time or it can happen immediately.

God even uses his resources to provide healing (2 Kings 2:19–22, salt and Ezekiel 47:8, fresh water). When Moses was preparing to turn the leadership over to Joshua, he sang a song, which exemplified not only his faith journey but also his ultimate trust that God is the source of healing.

> Now see that I, even I, am He, and there is no God besides Me; I kill and I make alive; I wound and I heal; Nor is there any who can deliver from My hand.
>
> Deuteronomy 32:39 (NKJV)

The Greek word for healing in this passage is "*Therapeuō*." This is where we get our English translation "therapeutics," which can best be explained as an attendant who cares for the sick; this is someone who treats a patient and is able to provide a cure, which will lead to the person's healing.

King Asa in 2 Chronicles 16 came down with a disease, and we are told that he did not seek the Lord to heal his feet. King Asa had been a prominent leader in Judah, but his problems began when he made a treaty with Ben-Hadad king of Syria, who dwelt in Damascus for his protection. God sent a seer (a prophet) named Hanani to confront Asa on his wrongdoings, but he wouldn't listen. He allowed anger to rise in his heart instead of seeking God first. Asa sought the physicians of his day for healing. His failure to seek God for national healing and for physical healing resulted in his sickness. This sickness would become so unbearable that he would eventually die.

When we look at historical accounts like this, we oftentimes become quick to judge. It's not always easy to trust God when facing life-changing circumstances. Judah had not experienced war in the previous thirty-five years, and now Asa would be faced with a national crisis. Recently, I was diagnosed with myeloma. When my doctor informed me of the diagnosis, I immediately became terrified. I remember coming home and secretly went to the website to find out everything I could find out about this cancer. The more I read, the more I panicked. I couldn't sleep, and I lived in fear. I remember trying to pray, but I was overwhelmed with the doctor's assessment and what I'd read on the Internet.

One day, as I was serving at church, I walked to our local pharmacy to get some sleeping pills, and when I returned, Brother Jimmy happened to be in our church lobby. Jimmy had previously gone through hip surgery, and then soon after, he was diagnosed with hepatitis C. He was told that if he didn't get a liver transplant, he would die. After he had gone back and forth to the hospital numerous times waiting for a suitable liver, he eventually got his transplant. The doctors said it was simply amazing how successful the surgery went, but they were even more amazed at his recovery.

While the two of us sat in the lobby that day, I asked him, "Brother Jimmy, how did you cope with the realization that you were facing near death?" Now you need to know Brother Jimmy. He's not one to dazzle you with a ton of scriptures. In fact, he serves as one of our ushers, and one of his duties is to collect the offering each week. Every time he is able to serve in this capacity, he always begins by telling our church family that God loves them and he loves them too. His answer to me was just as profound. He said, "Pastor, I just keep giving it to the Lord."

I am humbled once again. I have been in full-time ministry for more than twenty-five years, and I realized it was time for growth in my life once again. God was at work in my life perfecting me as a child of God and in my ministry calling. I began to do just as Brother Jimmy has modeled to me. Every time fear tried to set in my heart, I would give it to God. Since giving it to God, I have had a Positron Emission Tomography (PET) scan, which is an imaging test that can help reveal how your tissues and organs are functioning. A small amount of radioactive material is necessary to show this activity, and praise God, the result showed that there was *no* activity going on! All I can say is to God be all the glory!

God is the divine source of our healing, and he loves it when we call out to him.

> O LORD my God, I cried out to You, and You healed me.
>
> Psalm 30:2 (NKJV)

Jesus Christ Is Our Mediator

If we understand that God is the divine source of healing in the Old Testament, then let's understand how Jesus Christ is our (Jehovah *Rapha*) healer in the New Testament. It is interesting to note that this is one description of Jesus Christ that does not emphasize a title. In fact, there is no New Testament name for Jesus as healer. It's about what he *does*! (Proverbs 27:21, NKJV), says, "A man is valued by what others say of him." During Jesus's three years of ministry walking on this earth, those who knew him couldn't keep quiet. Those who trusted him as well as those who hated him were so astounded that they had to tell others about the healing ministry of Jesus. Jesus Christ glorifies his Father, and we can as well when we walk in obedience to his commands (supernaturally, or as a physician or attendant). Solomon, in his reflections in Ecclesiastes 3:3, reminds us that there is a time to heal. We must never think that we can heal anyone outside the power of God and the manifestation and the demonstration of the Holy Spirit working in our lives. Jesus, God's son, said, "I can of Myself do nothing" (John 5:30, NKJV). In context, Jesus was saying he has life in himself like his Father, and his one purpose is to glorify his Father. Because his Father likes to heal, so does his Son (and so should we).

While Jesus may use you or I to bring, administer, or be an agent of healing, we respond to his healing command with humble obedience. He does not *need* us, but we do need him, so remember that Jesus, our Lord has the appointed right to judge the living and the dead to eternal life or eternal judgment, and he also has the appointed right to heal.

When Jesus began his ministry in Galilee, he preached a sermon in his hometown of Nazareth, and they rejected him. However, this did not deter the life-giving exchange of Jesus's healing ministry (Luke 4:14–20, NKJV). After his departure, he began to cast out demons and performed other miracles (Matthew 4:23, NKJV). Soon, he would be in Simon Peter's house and would heal Peter's mother-in-law of a fever.

Then He got up and left the synagogue, and entered Simon's home. Now Simon's mother-in-law was suffering from a high fever, and they asked Him to help her. And standing over her, He rebuked the fever, and it left her; and she immediately got up and waited on them (Luke 4:38 (NKJV).

This was only the beginning! The Scriptures teach us that the healing ministry of Jesus was commonplace, and it was not limited to a time or day. I believe the demonstration of this power in Jesus Christ our Lord was directly connected to the closeness he shared with his Father. Jesus and God are one, and therefore Jesus's diligence in seeking his Father was a part of his DNA. He (Jesus) flowed in supernatural demonstrations of the Holy Spirit's anointing in which many would encounter healings. Remember, Jesus Christ our Lord loved to heal and so should we.

> When the sun was setting, all those who had any that were sick with various diseases brought them to Him; and He laid His hands on every one of them and healed them.
>
> (Luke 4:40, NKJV)

The Holy Spirit Empowers Us

The Holy Spirit gives us the power of God to heal in Jesus's name. Yes, the triune Godhead works together to accomplish his will for our lives for the advancement of his kingdom. In John 14, Jesus promises something that is nothing short of astounding. After performing countless miracles, healings, bringing the dead to life, and greater works than had ever been seen on earth, Jesus says that we who believe in him would do greater works than even he had done. Our minds cannot conceive of such a thing! How is it possible that this could be true? Jesus answers this question as follows:

Most assuredly, I say to you, he who believes in Me, the works that I do he will do also; and greater works than these he will do, because I go to My Father. And whatever you ask in My name, that I will do, that the Father may be glorified in the Son. If you ask anything in My name, I will do it. If you love Me, keep My commandments. And I will pray the Father, and He will give you another Helper, that He may abide with you forever—the Spirit of truth, whom the world cannot receive, because it neither sees Him nor knows Him; but you know Him, for He dwells with you and will be in you. I will not leave you orphans; I will come to you.

John 14:12–18 (NKJV)

Whatever we ask in Jesus's name, he will do it! And the Father has sent our helper, the Holy Spirit! Everything that we receive must come through Jesus. He's the one! He is our mediator who sits at God's side and makes intercessions for us (Romans 8:34). He's the one who baptizes us in the Holy Spirit. He's the One who prays to the Father on our behalf. He's the one who promised the Holy Spirit and all of the gifts of the Spirit.

But you shall receive power when the Holy Spirit has come upon you; and you shall be witnesses to

Me in Jerusalem, and in all Judea and Samaria, and to the end of the earth.

Acts 1:8 (NKJV)

I believe it is prudent to deter our quest in understanding healing for a moment so that we can set aside a few pages to understanding the Holy Spirit. I daresay the Holy Spirit is the most misunderstood personhood of the Trinity. This grave and rampant misunderstanding of the Holy Spirit has greatly damaged the desire of many believers to operate in the gifts of the Spirit. When the pews of the local church are filled with believers who are afraid to operate in the Spirit, the gifts of the Spirit are seldom manifested. When the gifts of the Spirit are seldom manifested, the world suffers greatly. What a profound loss for both the local church and the lost world!

We don't have to look far to identify why so many believers fear operating in the Spirit. Modern-day portrayals of the Holy Spirit are so far from the truth it grieves me greatly. A New York Times bestseller, endorsed even by some Christian organizations, portrays the Holy Spirit as a fluttering, speechless, fairy-like being. This doesn't remotely resemble the boldness of the one who was present in Acts!

> And when they had prayed, the place where they were assembled together was shaken; and they were all filled with the Holy Spirit, and they spoke the word of God with boldness.

> Acts 4:31 (NKJV)

Nor does it resemble the baptism of fire promised by John the Baptist:

> John answered, saying to all, "I indeed baptize you with water; but One mightier than I is coming, whose sandal strap I am not worthy to loose. He will baptize you with the Holy Spirit and fire."

> Luke 3:16 (NKJV)

I'm sure you have heard, as I have, the horror stories of those supposedly led by the Spirit into babbling and frothing at the mouth, disrupting worship services all around the world. This representation of the Spirit completely contradicts the Scriptures' instructions to the church of Corinth.

> Let all things be done decently and in order.

> 1 Corinthians 14:40 (NKJV)

I have seen so many dead, lifeless portrayals of the Spirit, too many to list out here. The overwhelming conclusion is much that is attributed to the Holy Spirit is not of the Holy Spirit at all. This should sadden our hearts and bring us to repentance over this misrepresentation of the Holy Spirit.

In this daunting endeavor, I can only give you out of what the Holy Spirit has given me. Scripture: in 1 Corinthians 12:3 (NASB), that no one can say, "Jesus is Lord" except by the Holy Spirit.

Tiffany was in Children's Church when she came to know the person of the Holy Spirit.

She says, "In children's church, I encountered the Holy Spirit for the first time. I will never forget it. They were showing a film portraying the crucifixion of Christ. I was so overcome with the awareness of my own sinfulness that I sobbed and sobbed and sobbed. I didn't care who was around me. I was completely inconsolable. No one could tell me what a good girl I was, or how at the young age of five, I couldn't have sinned that badly. The Holy Spirit had revealed to me what a sinner I was, that I needed a Savior, and that Jesus Christ had died for my sins, for me! In that moment, I became aware of the depths of God's great love for me. Oh, how he loves us! For many nights, I stayed up, crying tears of joy. When my sister asked me why I was crying, I told her it was because God loves me so much! It was undeniable. The Holy Spirit had done a work in me and brought me to the saving knowledge of my Lord and Savior, Jesus Christ. He had placed a seal on my heart for eternity."

> In Him you also trusted, after you heard the word of truth, the gospel of your salvation; in whom also, having believed, you were sealed with the Holy Spirit of promise, who is the guarantee of our inheritance until the redemption of the purchased possession, to the praise of His glory.
>
> Ephesians 1:13–14 (NASB)

"For that reason, and that reason alone, I would've been forever indebted to the Holy Spirit. He didn't need to do another thing for me ever again to prove the perfection and beauty of who he is! I was drawn to worship God with everything in me.

"After a time, I reached a point where I felt like I had used every good, perfect, glorifying word I knew to worship God. I felt like I had sung every song, praised with everything I knew, and it wasn't enough. Looking back, it seems laughable that I would think, at nine years old, that there weren't any good words or songs left in the English language that I hadn't already used in worship! But the Holy Spirit was stirring up in me a desire, a hunger, for more of him. I could hardly eat or sleep. After every Sunday service, I would run to the altar week after week for prayer. I wanted more intimacy, a deeper level of worship, as deep cries out to deep, I was desperate for more of his presence!

"One weekend, my family went to a revival service in Washington, DC. I sensed the power of the Holy Spirit was in that place, and I ran forward for prayer. A group of people prayed over me, and then, they moved on to someone else. I was determined not to leave until this hunger deep within me was satisfied. So I moved to another line to be prayed for again. Another group of people prayed over me and then moved on. So I moved to another line for prayer again. This continued until I was the last person left in the building, sitting in the middle of the front row of that sanctuary, with no one left to pray for me. A young boy came and found me and told me my mom was looking everywhere for me. So I reluctantly left the sanctuary.

"The next morning, I sat on my couch, weeping. I couldn't explain the hunger that the Holy Spirit had stirred up in me. And I couldn't satisfy it. All I could do was weep. I'll never forget that morning. My mom was vacuuming the living room floor. She asked me why I was crying. I tried to explain through sobbing breaths what I hardly understood myself. I tried to tell her that I didn't know any more words that were good enough to worship God with. I knew I wasn't making any sense. I barely understood myself! Without turning the vacuum off, without even looking up at me, from across the room, my mom said, 'Well then speak in it.' I opened my mouth, and out came the most beautiful words of worship to my God that I had ever heard. They poured out like rushing water. Everything that had been bottled up in me for so long poured out in a language I had never known before. The Holy Spirit had stirred up this hunger in me and had completely and utterly fulfilled it! It was complete perfection!

"God the Father is perfect! Jesus Christ is perfect! The Holy Spirit is perfect! There is no imperfection. No one can manufacture a move of the Spirit. No one can manipulate a move of the Spirit. No one can imitate of move of the Spirit. When the Holy Spirit moves, it is absolute perfection! There is nothing more beautiful than to witness an authentic move of the Holy Spirit. The local church has been greatly damaged by attempts to manufacture, manipulate, and imitate the Spirit. But once he shows up, there is no denying that there is none like our God! Oh, how the world desperately needs a genuine move of the Spirit!

"I recognize fully that not every Christian's encounters with the Holy Spirit are mechanically the same. I know that my experience with the Holy Spirit on my couch that morning is not the same as other believers' experiences. However, believe me when I say that I am nothing unique or special compared to other believers. There is nothing that God has given me that he would not give to another. And the mechanics of how it's given is completely up to God's sovereign plan. The only important thing is this: the Holy Spirit is looking for yielded vessels to accomplish God's kingdom work on this earth. God did not ask for vessels of silver or gold. He asked only for vessels that are yielded. When we are yielded to the Holy Spirit, we experience intimacy with Christ. When we are yielded to the Holy Spirit, we are able to worship God in spirit and in truth. When we are yielded to the Holy Spirit, we are used in God's kingdom work. The mechanics of how the Holy Spirit accomplishes that intimacy, that level of worship, are up to him. Too often we focus on the mechanics of how we believe something should be done or the specific gifts of the Spirit we believe are necessary and we miss the truth."

> God is Spirit, and those who worship Him must
> worship in spirit and truth.
>
> John 4:24 (NASB)

"Finally, I will bring you to the moment the Holy Spirit revealed to me that I would be called into a healing ministry. I was in college and had decided to go with a group of friends and family down to Florida. There was a revival in Florida that we had heard about, so we decided to go there for spring break. We witnessed many miracles, healings, and people being saved while we were there. It was unlike anything I had ever seen before. During the day, we would wait in line on the sidewalk outside of the church so that we could get a seat for the service that night. One day, when it wasn't my turn to wait in line, I went in for a time of prayer in the church. I will never forget that day. I was walking around the church praying with my eyes closed. As I was walking, the Holy Spirit revealed to me that I would be used in a healing ministry. I fell to my knees and wept for hours. I cried out to God in a painful cry, almost a groaning. I found myself crying out, 'Lord, save them! Lord, save them!' I couldn't stop. It was as if the Holy Spirit had allowed me, for a moment, to see a glimpse of God's compassion for the lost, and it completely wrecked me—I couldn't even stand up. I was leaning against a pole, and when I could finally lift up my head, hours later, I saw that the pole I had been leaning on was attached to a flag. The flag read, 'SOULS.'"

> But when He saw the multitudes, He was moved with compassion for them, because they were weary and scattered, like sheep having no shepherd.
>
> Matthew 9:36 (NKJV)

"The Holy Spirit had shown me from the very beginning that the healing ministry God had called me to wasn't about healing…it was about souls. To minimize a healing ministry to anything less than eternal unity with God is taking God's purpose and power out of the ministry."

> But when the multitudes knew it, they followed Him; and He received them and spoke to them about the kingdom of God, and healed those who had need of healing.
>
> Luke 9:11 (NKJV)

> And one of them, when he saw that he was healed, returned, and with a loud voice glorified God, and fell down on his face at His feet, giving Him thanks. And he was a Samaritan.
>
> Luke 17:15–16 (NKJV)

> Then Peter said, "Silver and gold I do not have, but what I do have I give you: In the name of Jesus Christ of Nazareth, rise up and walk." And he took him by the right hand and lifted him up, and immediately his feet and ankle bones received strength. So he, leaping up, stood and walked and entered the temple with them—

walking, leaping, and praising God. And all the people saw him walking and praising God. Then they knew that it was he who sat begging alms at the Beautiful Gate of the temple; and they were filled with wonder and amazement at what had happened to him.

Acts 3:6–10 (NKJV)

A genuine move of the Holy Spirit leads the lost to Christ. The focus is always our eternal well-being. The gifts of the Spirit—signs and wonders, healings, miracles—none are meant for the purposes of temporary, earthly pleasure. None of the spiritual gifts are meant to be sought after as prideful gain. Nor are they meant to be put up on pedestals as idols and worshiped. Instead, they serve a far superior purpose—to bear witness of so great a salvation! Oh, how God's purposes are better than our own! They are all meant to bring glory to God and eternal salvation to our lost and dying world.

Therefore we must give the more earnest heed to the things we have heard, lest we drift away. For if the word spoken through angels proved steadfast, and every transgression and disobedience received a just reward, how shall we escape if we neglect so great a salvation, which at the first began to be spoken by the Lord, and was confirmed to us by those who heard Him, God also bearing witness both with signs and wonders, with various miracles, and gifts of the Holy Spirit, according to His own will?

Hebrews 2:1–4 (NKJV)

But now I go away to Him who sent Me, and none of you asks Me, "Where are You going?" But because I have said these things to you, sorrow has filled your heart. Nevertheless I tell you the truth. It is to your advantage that I go away; for if I do not go away, the Helper will not come to you; but if I depart, I will send Him to you. And when He has come, He will convict the world of sin, and of righteousness, and of judgment: of sin, because they do not believe in Me; of righteousness, because I go to My Father and you see Me no more; of judgment, because the ruler of this world is judged. I still have many things to say to you, but you cannot bear them now. However, when He, the Spirit of truth, has come, He will guide you into all truth; for He will not speak on His own authority, but whatever He hears He will speak; and He will tell you things to come. He will glorify Me, for He will take of what is Mine and declare it to you. All things that the Father has are Mine. Therefore I said that He will take of Mine and declare it to you.

John 16:5–15 (NKJV)

We are in a dangerous time, church—a time when imitators of the Holy Spirit run rampant, making it much more difficult for many local churches to be yielded to genuine moves of the Spirit. But, we are also in an exciting time, church! It's a time when all of the things that happened in the early church in the Book of Acts are being restored to the church today! As we gain a greater understanding of God's will for healing, I implore you to yield to the Holy Spirit—he never disappoints! If I didn't believe that the Holy Spirit was this book, I wouldn't form a single word. We could pen the same words, with the same sentence structures in the same paragraphs as many other authors, but the power is in the Holy Spirit! In my experience with the Holy Spirit, I have found that when it's genuine, people are changed by it. Words on a page cannot do that. Only a genuine encounter with the Holy Spirit can allow us to truly understand healing.

Why Healing Is Necessary

L et me interject here for our understanding of why healing is necessary. Remember that God does not need to justify why He allows sickness, and he definitely doesn't need our permission for his actions. We must also remember that he is *just* in all he does. After receiving the law from God in Deuteronomy 32:3–4 (NKJV), Moses declares, "For I proclaim the name of the LORD: Ascribe greatness to our God. He is the Rock, His work is perfect; For all His ways are justice, a God of truth and without injustice; righteous and upright is He." Isaiah 55:9 reminds us that God's ways are higher than ours.

So the bottom line here is that healing is necessary because the ultimate will of God is to advance his kingdom through victory over the world until the ultimate time of Christ's return in glory. I realize that the older I get, the richer my focus becomes. I'm getting a purer kingdom focus. Many in Christendom are consumed with the kingdoms of this world. I've seen many stray away from what's important to God as they chased bigger houses, more money, women, men, and all the pleasures of this world. They begin to isolate themselves by distancing themselves from Godly counsel, putting stress on meaningful relationships, and most saddening, not fulfilling God's calling on their lives. Interestingly enough, they can't live with themselves, nor can they live with others. They are simply miserable. Proverbs 18:1 (NKJV) says, "A man who isolates himself seeks his own desire; He rages against all wise judgment." When you live your life with a focus on God's kingdom, then your values are shifted and your life is consumed with how others can know the Father. How can we bring healing through the power of the empty cross? How can we, in our time here on earth, tell others about the saving grace found in Jesus Christ our Lord?

Reasons for Sickness and Disease

Here are some reasons for sickness and disease:

1. Sin is the primary reason. This all began with the fall of Adam (Genesis 3). Therefore, all humanity has a fallen nature with human bodies, and these bodies are prone to sickness and disease. The good news is that when a person makes Jesus Christ his or her Lord and Savior, they are given a new "divine nature," thus becoming overcomers of the ultimate penalty of sin—separation from God's presence. But we can also conclude from Paul's letter to the Ephesians that we have been given a new nature that supersedes the old nature resulting in victory over sin and disease.

And you He made alive, who were dead in trespasses and sins, in which you once walked according to the course of this world, according to the prince of the power of the air, the spirit who now works in the sons of disobedience, among whom also we all once conducted ourselves in the lusts of our flesh, fulfilling the desires of the flesh and of the mind, and were by nature children of wrath, just as the others. "But God, who is rich in mercy, because of His great love with which He loved us, even when we were dead in trespasses, made us alive together with Christ (by grace you have been saved), and raised us up together, and made us sit together in the heavenly places in Christ Jesus, that in the ages to come He might show the exceeding riches of His grace in His kindness toward us in Christ Jesus.

(Ephesians 2:1–7, NKJV)

I love this phrase: "But God." Because of God's love and faithfulness toward us, He has made a way for us to be made whole. In other words, God has made a way for us to live an abundant life with him and in a redeemed relationship with him once again because of his sacrifice of his one and only Son who was the perfect, spotless Lamb of God. God is able beyond all human imagination and is competent to save the worst of sinners. All anyone must do is place his or her faith in the life, death, and resurrection of Jesus Christ. Have faith in Jesus Christ who gave his life on the cross in order that we might be reconciled back to God—restored, healed, whole! That is God's will for all, not for some—all of humanity. Humanity blew it, but God who is "rich in mercy" made a way. Hallelujah!

2. God's judgment of our immoral or unethical behavior (punishment). Hebrews 12:5–11 teaches us that God will discipline his children to bring correction. He does this because his nature is divine and he disciplines his children to align them to his divine nature. In Psalm 119, we see a progression where the psalmist grows closer to God and values the life God gave him in response to the Lord's discipline. First, we see that this person, because of his sin nature, did his own thing. But something happened. He put his faith, hope, and trust in God. There was a change! He began to lean on God's word. In these days they turned to the Torah, which contains the first five books of the Old Testament. These were the central teachings, statutes, and precepts of God to man. While he leaned on God's Holy Word, he learned that God would protect him from the enemy. He was committed to a growing relationship with his God.

Before I was afflicted I went astray, but now I keep Your word. You are good, and do good; Teach me Your statutes. The proud have forged a lie against me, but I will keep Your precepts with my whole heart. Their heart is as fat as grease, but I delight in Your law. It is good for me that I have been afflicted, That I may learn Your statutes. The law of Your mouth is better to me than thousands of coins of gold and silver. Your hands have made me and fashioned me; Give me understanding, that I may learn Your commandments. Those who fear You will be glad when they see me, Because I have hoped in Your word. I know, O Lord, that Your judgments are right, And that in faithfulness You have afflicted me.

Psalm 119:67–75 (NKJV)

I remember when I did not know the Lord, I did a lot of foolish things. I lived my life on my own terms. "But God" changed all that.

Here's my story:

I grew up in Plainfield, New Jersey, in a home with a dad and mom but did not have a spiritual role model. My teen years consisted of promiscuous living filled with drinking, drugs, thievery, and on and on (I am sure you see the picture). I grew up very much afraid of my dad, especially when he was high or drunk. I remember very vividly when I was sixteen, he kicked my brother and me out of the house while shooting at us with a 32-caliber pistol. In 1980, at the age of eighteen, I joined the United States Marine Corps.

While serving my country, I continued to live a destructive life, doing many illegal activities. My behavior for the first five years of my Marine Corps career was worse than my previous years as a teenager. I learned to beat the system, because in my job, I was privy to when random drug tests were being given. I continued to party a few more years away, not realizing how bad it was, but that all began to change in 1983.

While stationed at Willow Grove, Pennsylvania, I met a young lady who was also there on active duty. Willow Grove is a military installation where reservists are trained, primarily on weekends. This duty required me to work many weekends. This female Marine (now my wife) and a very close friend of ours persistently invited me to the Base Chapel for Sunday services. Finally, during the Easter season of 1984, at the age of twenty-two, I decided to accept their invitation to go to the Base Chapel. It was at that service that God began to penetrate my heart deeply. I realized where my life was headed and soon became very uneasy and somewhat afraid of the future. I still denied, rejected, and fought this feeling, resulting in no remorse or change of heart at that time.

I knew about God and Jesus because I had spent some time growing up in church.

A few months later, around June of 1985, one morning while I was lying in bed, I heard a voice. This voice was very distinct to me; while not audible, it was penetrating through every fabric of my heart, mind, and soul. This voice said, "Kurt, you have heard it before, but now, if you do not receive my Son, Jesus Christ, as your Lord and Savior, you are going to die and go to hell." This was very real to me! I immediately felt sorrowful for what I was doing with my life, and I wanted the change. You see, I had known about Jesus and that he had died for me, but I had refused to respond to him. This spiritual confrontation got my attention. I knew I had to make a choice. Life, its meaning, my purpose—everything was very confusing. But through God's silent yet unmistakably clear voice, I began to realize how much he loves me. That morning, I cried like a baby as I accepted Jesus in my life. I asked him to come into my heart. I asked him to change my heart, my life, everything. He did it! I am still not perfect, and I have many challenges. I have learned that I need to trust him every day in all circumstances. Jesus gives me strength for the new challenges I face with each new day. I have come to believe in my heart that God really does love me. Romans 5:8 (NKJV), remind us, "But God demonstrates His own love toward us, in that while we were still sinners, Christ died for us."

Since receiving Jesus as Lord of my life, many things have changed (my values, my dreams, my relationships, and much more, for the better). I have a strong desire to both love God and love others. I have learned how to forgive others when they have hurt me. I forgave my father for all the abuse that I received for so many years. Now my dad and I share a respectful relationship, and I take every opportunity to tell him about the forgiveness that is found in knowing Christ, even for his sins. I am praying that one day, he will accept Christ and share in the joy that I now have. I have learned to look to God for strength when making tough decisions, like when I quit smoking. I used to smoke two to three packs a day for more than eight years. I also gave up drugs. I trusted God to change me. Even my vocabulary changed. I used to use explicit crude and vulgar words not fitting for any ears to hear, and God even took care of my language problem. As I said earlier, I know I am not perfect, but I serve a God who is. I know I can trust God as I follow Jesus.

In cases where a believer is overtaken in his or her sin, and rebellion continues to occur due to his or her own selfish will, God can terminate that life early if He so chooses.

If anyone sees his brother sinning a sin which does not lead to death, he will ask, and He will give him life for those who commit sin not leading to death. There is sin leading to death. I do not say that he should pray about that. All unrighteousness is sin, and there is sin not leading to death.

1 John 5:16–17 (NKJV)

The Apostle Paul addresses the people of Rome about immoral behavior, and because of the willful choices that some of them were making, God allowed them to be overtaken with some terrible effects that caused pain and suffering (see Romans 1:20–26, NKJV).

3. God permits affliction to glorify himself (example: the Book of Job). It is important to know that God does not always allow sickness to teach us something. In Job's case, Satan thought God's righteous servant would deny God if he (Satan) could inflict physical and emotional pain. But Job's faith in the will of God was far superior, and God would be glorified. This is a case where God's omniscience prevailed. Satan thought he knew more about Job than God did. Praise God that he knows infinitely more than Satan, the accuser.

But He knows the way that I take; When He has tested me, I shall come forth as gold. My foot has held fast to His steps; I have kept His way and not turned aside. I have not departed from the commandment of His lips; I have treasured the words of His mouth more than my necessary food. But He is unique, and who can make Him change? And whatever His soul desires, that He does. For He performs what is appointed for me, and many such things are with Him.

Job 23:10–14 (NKJV)

4. God allows sickness to keep us humble. In 2 Corinthians 12:7 (NKJV), we find that the Apostle Paul had a sickness which was not a result of an act of sin on his part: "And lest I should be exalted above measure by the abundance of the revelation, a thorn in the flesh was given to me, a messenger of Satan to buffet me, lest I be exalted above measure." Paul didn't know why he had this condition, and he even asked the Lord three times to take it away before he accepted God's will for this sickness. The Lord responded to Paul's prayer by saying, "My grace is sufficient for you, for My strength is made perfect in weakness" (2 Corinthians 12:9, NKJV). We can also come to the conclusion that we are fallen human beings with human bodies prone to sickness and disease.

As I said earlier in my story, I served twenty years in the United States Marine Corps. As a part of staying mentally and physically prepared to defend our great country, my endurance training consisted of intensive exercise at least three times a week. For the most part, I ran every day to prepare for the company runs. During this tenure, I also ran the Marine Corps Marathon twice—26.2 miles. After I retired from the Marine Corps, I found that I had high cholesterol. At one point, it was as high as 272. I was basically a walking time bomb. My high cholesterol developed over a period of time from eating what we called chow hall food and every other fast food available. Over time, my arteries began to calcify, and now there remains some scar tissues that are there for life (I still believe the Lord can remove the scar tissues). These scar tissues affect blood flow. Since retiring from the military in 2000, I have been seeing my doctor twice a year. At one point, my doctor had me on forty milligrams of Lipitor, a drug to help lower cholesterol. I remember asking my doctor how long I had to take the medicine, and her response was, "For life." My response to her was something like, "No way, God is going to take care of this."

In 2008, God spoke to me through his word and gave me my breakthrough. The passage, found in 1 Thessalonians 5:23 (NKJV), says, "Now may the God of peace Himself sanctify you completely; and may your whole spirit, soul, and body be preserved blameless at the coming of our Lord Jesus Christ." It was at this moment that I began to pray and fast for my healing. I recognized that I could not pursue my healing by being one-dimensional. This verse became a life verse for me. I made it my aim to be healthy tridimensionally—spirit, soul, and body. Slowly, my bad cholesterol numbers began to decline and so did my Lipitor dosage—from forty down to twenty milligrams. I began to pray with fasting, and I began to take assessments of myself to get to know this person God created by his design. I began to allow the Holy Spirit to reveal my heart issues through his word. I began to see areas in my character and my personality that I had to allow God to work in; I also began to eat healthy and refrained from consuming fast food, sugars, and sweets. In addition, I added exercise to my regimen, at minimum, an hour a day four days a week.

In 2010, I went to the doctor just after finishing a twenty-one-day Daniel fast. The doctor read my test results from my latest blood work and asked in a startled tone, "What have you been doing?"

I thought she was chastising me, so I said, "Why, what's the matter?"

She said, "Nothing is wrong. Your total cholesterol level is down to 174 [under 200 is desirable], your HDL [good] cholesterol was in the excellent range and the

LDL [bad] cholesterol was reduced significantly and in a good range." She added, "Whatever you are doing, keep doing it."

Since then, I continue to live my life verse (1 Thessalonians 5:23), and my Lipitor dosage has been reduced to ten milligrams for maintenance, and my levels are still amazingly good. I believe that God allowed this sickness to draw me closer to him. I am continually drawn to the goodness of God. I have learned to trust him more and more as I walk through this healing journey with him. I thank God for using this sickness to the aid of transforming my total spirit, soul and body to the image of his Son. Thank you, Holy Spirit, for the indescribable work you do in the human heart!

Hezekiah became king in Judah at the age of twenty-five (1 Kings 18:1, 2 Chronicles 29), and he reigned for twenty-nine years. He was a great leader in Judah. He began his reign by restoring worship in the temple. He led the priests and Levites in a time of repentance and restoration in the house of the Lord. This was a spectacular time! Worship was restored, the high places and altars where the people of God were worshipping foreign gods were destroyed, and the hearts of the people worshipped the Lord God once again. The Bible says, "Thus Hezekiah did throughout all Judah, and he did what was good and right and true before the LORD his God. And in every work that he began in the service of the house of God, in the law and in the commandment, to seek his God, he did it with all his heart. So he prospered" (2 Chronicles 31:20–21, NKJV).

Near the close of his reign, King Hezekiah got a life-ending sickness, and he prayed to God for healing. God had given Hezekiah a word through Isaiah the prophet to get his affairs in order because he was going to die (2 Kings 20:1). Hezekiah was not ready to die. He was doing great things for God and enjoying the favor and blessings for his work. So Hezekiah turned to the prophet Isaiah and asked him to intercede for him. The response was that God heard his prayers and would add fifteen years to his life. He would confirm this through a miracle. God would heal him by giving him a sign that the shadow of the sundial of Ahaz, which would lengthen down the eastern steps in the afternoon, but God would cause the sundial to go backwards ten degrees; thus, Hezekiah was healed. This would have been a great ending to this king's service, but God saw something undone in Hezekiah's character. The people and nations around Hezekiah heard of his victories, his intercession for the people, his restoration work, and now his healing. Many gifts and treasures were given to him, but he would become prideful and begin to display all his treasures to foreigners. This displeased the Lord, and now discipline would come as a result of this lack of humility. God would take all his possessions, all that he had accumulated and give them over to Babylon, and Judah would go into captivity, leaving only a remnant. You say, why so severe? This is the extent, which God will go to keep one man's heart pure. Hezekiah did repent, and God remained faithful to his promise to heal and give Hezekiah an additional fifteen years to his life. I believe those last fifteen years were more valuable than all his previous years, because now he knew true humility.

Hindrances

There are many hindrances that keep us from being healed. Hindrances slow down and, in some cases, block the flow of God's healing virtues. Hezekiah's was pride. He became very arrogant and self-righteous which led to his downfall. Pride is dangerous because other people end up getting hurt and the one causing the pain often doesn't realize it or doesn't even care because they are self-absorbed. Proverbs 29:3 (NKJV), says, "A man's pride will bring him low, but the humble in spirit will retain honor." Paul instructs Timothy to carefully observe those appointed to senior leadership because they can easily become conceited and come under the "same condemnation as the devil" (1 Timothy 3:6 (NKJV). Pride is very dangerous. It is a sickness that needs to be rid of. Pride keeps you from God altogether. Pride is deceptive and causes people to make choices that hurt them and others often times in the name of God.

Another hindrance is an unhealthy fear of the Lord. A healthy fear is one where God is revered; he is respected not only for who he is but what he has done. People tend to have an unhealthy fear because they don't believe that God is who says he is and that he can do all that the Scriptures teach and reveal about him. Moses instructed Israel, as they were about to pass into the Promised Land, to remember to keep God's statutes and judgments, which gave evidence that they feared the Lord. This fear was to declare that their allegiance was to God alone and they were to trust that God would take care of them.

> Now this is the commandment, and these are the statutes and judgments which the Lord your God has commanded to teach you, that you may observe them in the land which you are crossing over to possess, that you may fear the

Lord your God, to keep all His statutes and His commandments which I command you, you and your son and your grandson, all the days of your life, and that your days may be prolonged.

Deuteronomy 6:1–2 (NKJV)

Remember, God loves you, and everything he does is for our good. His statutes and judgments are for our protection as well as our longevity, health, and well-being. Solomon was the wisest king in the Bible. He got to a point in his life where he got bored and began to use his throne for personal pleasures. His actions truly show the frailty of man and the condition of our heart. After he had "sowed his wild oaks," he came to this conclusion: "Let us hear the conclusion of the whole matter: Fear God and keep His commandments, for this is man's all. 14 For God will bring every work into judgment, including every secret thing, whether good or evil" (Ecclesiastes 12:13–14, NKJV).

Doubt is another hindrance. Doubt is to have uncertainty. It causes you to hesitate. You want to believe, but there are obstacles playing in your mind that keep you from trusting God for your healing. Two obstructions that cause doubt are time and effort. How much time do you spend in prayer and the word of God? Doubt creeps in when we listen to other influences that don't have an allegiance to God and Jesus Christ. They don't believe in the Holy Spirit that has promised to walk along side of us. When Peter and the rest of the disciples were on a boat in the middle of the Sea of Galilee they saw Jesus coming, walking on the water, and they were afraid. The only one who had a little courage was Peter. He said to Jesus, "Lord, if it is You, command me to come to You on the water" (Matthew 12:28, (NKJV). So Jesus did just as Peter asked, but when the waves started swaying a little harder, Peter got scared (now, we need to give Peter a little more props, at least he was willing to get out of the boat). After he got out of the boat and started walking toward the Lord, but for a brief moment, he took his eyes off Jesus and began to sink. So Jesus reached out his hand and grabbed Peter and said to him, "O you of little faith, why did you doubt?" (Matthew 12:31, NKJV). To overcome doubt, we need to keep our eyes fixed on Jesus. This is not always easy, but it is a discipline you can master.

The Gift of Healing Is Available Today

The good news is that those who have placed their faith in the Lord Jesus Christ can walk in this anointed spiritual gift too. But the key to unleashing the power of the gift is the same as it was for Jesus: "diligence in seeking Him [God the Father]." In other words, how much time do you, as a believer, spend seeking him, abiding in him, trusting him, and obeying him? I find in many circles today, many Christ-followers spend more time feverishly talking and debating about the gifts of the Spirit versus responsively *doing* the ministry of the gifts. In Matthew 10, when Jesus sent out the twelve disciples, he gave specific instructions for his disciples to carry on in his healing ministry in juxtaposition with sharing the gospel. Remember, healing is used to bring glory to God through Jesus Christ and to fulfill our Creator's purpose. I must emphasize that healing is for today.

The church should expect a resurgence of supernatural signs and wonders to coincide with her repentance and recommitment to the gospel of Jesus Christ. Faithful followers of Jesus Christ should commit to the understanding and employment of their spiritual gifts in the body and for the body. The element that clogs the flow of God's restoring work is a failure to abide in him. When we abide in him, we are transformed not only in his image but also in the demonstration of his power. The elephant in the room is when we straddle the fence allowing our attitudes and actions to be embedded in sin nature and yet wanting to operate in the spiritual nature. This has not and will not work.

The Catholic Church has struggled with this for centuries as they continue to come to agreement to the process of sainthood. Their bottom line measurement to sainthood is the validation of whether a miracle was performed by the person being canonized regardless of their character, conduct or how they served God's people. A recent article by the International Movement, "We

Are Church," states, "The International Movement We Are Church believes that beatification and ultimately sainthood should not be measured by whether a "miracle" can be attributed to a particular person, but rather, whether someone's life truly embodies the values of Christ who sought, not power, but the well being of God's people."[4] I must say their assessment in this matter is very shallow as it relies more on the ability of man than the power of God. There are some in the evangelical circles that have found it appealing to falsely manifest healings and miracles to bring attention to themselves and ultimately increase revenue. The Church today is coming into a season where signs and wonders are being released as a response to faithful followers of Jesus Christ who are committed to God's transformation in those areas we don't like to address (character, morality, and ethics). This season, I believe, will usher in the return of our Lord for his bride as we respond by carrying out the specific orders he gave his disciples as they went out to advance God's kingdom agenda:

> Heal the sick, raise the dead, cleanse the lepers, cast out demons. Freely you received, freely give.
>
> Matthew 10:8 (NASB)

Notice what Jesus said and what he didn't say. He didn't say, "Think about it" or "Analyze it." He didn't say, "Do a study about it" or "Strive for agreement." He didn't say, "Let's talk about this" or "Let's vote on this." Get the point? God has given Christ-followers authority to advance his kingdom in this earth through the healing ministry.

> And He called the twelve together, and gave them power and authority over all the demons and to heal diseases. And He sent them out to proclaim the kingdom of God and to perform healing.
>
> Luke 9:1 (NKJV)

> Most assuredly, I say to you, he who believes in Me, the works that I do he will do also; and greater works than these he will do, because I go to My Father. And whatever you ask in My name, that I will do, that the Father may be glorified in the Son.
>
> John 14:12–13 (NKJV)

> And He said to them, "Go into all the world and preach the gospel to every creature. He who believes and is baptized will be saved; but he who does not believe will be condemned. And these

signs will follow those who believe: In My name they will cast out demons; they will speak with new tongues; they will take up serpents; and if they drink anything deadly, it will by no means hurt them; they will lay hands on the sick, and they will recover."

Mark 16:15–18 (NKJV)

And I, brethren, when I came to you, did not come with excellence of speech or of wisdom declaring to you the testimony of God. For I determined not to know anything among you except Jesus Christ and Him crucified. I was with you in weakness, in fear, and in much trembling. And my speech and my preaching were not with persuasive words of human wisdom, but in demonstration of the Spirit and of power, that your faith should not be in the wisdom of men but in the power of God.

1 Corinthians 2:1–5 (NKJV)

In Acts 9:32, we are told that Peter was preaching the gospel, and in his travels, he headed toward Lydda. There, he found a man named Aeneas who had been bedridden for eight years, and he was paralyzed. Peter had a burden for this man to know the healing power of Jesus Christ. Peter had personally witnessed Jesus in action. He had gone through many hard knocks in his time with the

Lord, not to mention he had denied him three times. But now, this is a different Peter. He is filled with the Spirit with an undeniable faith in the healing power of Jesus the Christ, so much that he commands Aeneas to be healed in the authority and power in Jesus name.

> And Peter said to him, "Aeneas, Jesus the Christ heals you. Arise and make your bed." Then he arose immediately.
>
> Acts 9:34 (NKJV)

Peter was used by God to demonstrate his power. Notice that Peter did not say, "I heal you," but "Jesus the Christ heals you." Looking at the context of this passage, the church honored the Lord and each other; there was a genuine God-fearing culture that was ripe for this demonstration of God's power. The problem is, too many people are prideful, and when they attempt to do this divine work of God, they often want to draw attention to themselves rather than toward the purposes of God. God cannot use our self-pride. We must learn to walk humbly before him at all times, living in submission to his will and direction. Also, notice that Aeneas didn't waver—he got up and walked. There is something to be said about being obedient to God's instructions.

I remember attending my first healing conference in Kansas City, Missouri. Another brother and I were led to Kansas City to check out the International House of Prayer (IHOP). When we arrived, we had not known that we would be attending this conference. This was, as I called it, the icing on the cake. I sat there listening to Bill Johnson teach about the healing ministry of Jesus. He shared about how he was just a vehicle of God to teach others; he encouraged the audience to be sensitive to the needs around them and be obedient to praying for those whom the Holy Spirit led to be healed. Oftentimes, he said he would take a group of teens to the mall just to pray for people. There is nothing spooky about the healing ministry of Jesus. It's spiritually normal.

I remember coming to a time when we were invited to pray for healing of others in need at the conference. I prayed for a Korean woman who'd had a back problem all her life—she couldn't bend over. She was receiving the same instructions as I was by means of radio translation. This was my first encounter of praying for someone's healing with the understanding that God not only loves to heal, but that he wanted to use me. What made this encounter interesting is that the woman couldn't understand me, and I couldn't understand her. So we resorted to body language. I began to pray for this woman's healing as thousands of others were praying for healing for others. The room was filled with electricity! After about fifteen minutes, those who were prayed for were instructed to respond to the healing touch of Jesus through an action. I was amazed to see this woman bend over and touch her toes without inhibitions. She would rise up with a smile and tears of joy along with countless others who were receiving their touch from the Lord. Believe me, this changed my ministry. I have such a confidence in the healing power of Jesus!

In Numbers 20, Moses had received instruction to speak to the rock and have water come out for the people of Israel. Instead, he struck the rock and dishonored God. This one act caused him not to be able to cross over into the land of Canaan (see Numbers 20:9–12). God will not use any of our false pride or selfish efforts no matter how justified they appear.

When Peter and John were going to church to pray, they encountered a man who had a physical ailment since birth. This man got comfortable being sick, so he was in what I call the "accepted survival mode." All he wanted was some money so that he could eat another day. But look at Peter's response:

> But Peter said, "I do not possess silver and gold,
> but what I do have I give to you: In the name of
> Jesus Christ the Nazarene—walk!"
>
> Acts 3:6 (NKJV)

(Also, see Acts 4:30, Jeremiah 3:22, Jeremiah
6:14, Isaiah 6:10, and Hosea 7:1.)

In Acts 9, there is a righteous woman named Tabitha.
She had the gift of service and giving. The Bible tells
us that she became sick and died. Evidently, Tabitha's
life-giving ministry affected others around her. Fellow
disciples heard that Peter was in the town nearby and
implored Peter to come and pray for Tabitha (after she
had already died, I remind you). Talk about faith!

> But Peter put them all out, and knelt down
> and prayed. And turning to the body he said,
> "Tabitha, arise." And she opened her eyes, and
> when she saw Peter she sat up.
>
> Acts 9:40 (NKJV)

Faith Is Essential

As the believer exercises his or her healing ministry, they must be able to discern when there is a faith *void*. Healing, like other spiritual gifts, is stifled when there is doubt. The Bible gives us instruction that if someone in our congregation is sick, call the elders and have them pray. Failure to do this is a lack of faith.

> Is anyone among you sick? Let him call for the elders of the church, and let them pray over him, anointing him with oil in the name of the Lord. And the prayer of faith will save the sick, and the Lord will raise him up. And if he has committed sins, he will be forgiven.
>
> James 5:14–15 (NKJV)

Also within the church, God has given some the gift of healing. This too is crucial in how God chooses to manifest his glory. Because God is Spirit, he releases spiritual gifts to accomplish his plan (Romans 12:6–8, 1 Corinthians 12:1–12, and Ephesians 4:11–13). Don't be skittish—remember that God's word trumps experience. Your encounter with the Holy Spirit will never be at the mercy of a man with an argument. Your belief will determine your theology. Ask yourself, do you believe God heals? Do you believe that you have the power to heal in Jesus's name? What will be your response when you see someone healed in your sphere? What is your first response when you see someone in need of healing? Will you pray for them and command the sickness to leave, or will you have a "woe is me" discussion about it? Will you exercise your faith in God and trust him to use you to advance his kingdom?

In 2 Chronicles, we learn that King Asa had a bad attitude. He had made a decision that he would trust more in man than in God. So much that Hanani, a prophet, stated, "For the eyes of the LORD run to and fro throughout the whole earth, to show Himself strong on behalf of those whose heart is loyal to Him. In this you have done foolishly; therefore from now on you shall have wars" (2 Chronicles 16:9, NKJV). Asa got mad; he had more faith in man than in God, and he made it clear. In his later years, he got a disease in his feet, and in turn, he decided to seek out a doctor before he sought out the Lord.

In John 5, we read that Jesus went to Jerusalem for a feast (probably a Passover). In Jerusalem, there was a gate called the Sheep Gate. In Hebrew, this gate is called Bethesda, meaning "house of mercy for the cure." Many sick people—blind, lame, and paralyzed—would gather there waiting for the waters to be stirred by angels (this was truly a miraculous situation). There was a man there with a disease that prevented him from getting into the water before the others. He had been dealing with this illness for more than thirty-eight years. Sad to say, but he had settled in his situation. He had been sick for so long that he became feeble and grief began to set in. He lacked the strength to do anything. Jesus saw this man and asked him if he wanted to be healed "or do you just want to settle? Do you think this is all there is?" (my paraphrase). He said yes, but nobody would help him get into the water before the others. Jesus saw that this man wanted to be healed, and he knew that God would be glorified, so he did what was only right to do.

Jesus told the man to get up and walk (John 5:8). Take that step of faith toward your healing. The Jews got indignant because it was the Sabbath. No one was supposed to carry his or her mat on the Sabbath, go figure! When asked by the Jews who told him to carry his mat, he said that the man who healed him told him to pick up his mat and carry it. In other words, Jesus's words trumped the powerless laws of the Jews. People are not looking for another discussion, but the power and demonstration of God. My recent illness has caused me to take a step back to the point where I recognized myself saying, "I'm getting older, so just go with it." I'm supposed to be susceptible to illnesses as I get older. Well, that's a lie from the devil.

The thirty-eight years the man at the gate spent with illness is a long time of inactivity. This was a long time of not serving God. This man spent most of his life waiting for somebody else to do something for him. Everybody's mad at somebody because they didn't do something for him or her. Here's a word of wisdom: Don't wait until tomorrow to take a step of faith for your healing. "It is the Sabbath" (verse 9). Start by believing—declare the word of the Lord. Make that phone call, set up that appointment, sign up for that class, initiate forgiveness, repent and turn to Jesus. God is a God of second chances (see verses 14, 28–29).

So the Jews were saying to the man who was cured, "It is the Sabbath, and it is not permissible for you to carry your pallet."

John 5:10 (NKJV)

Now let me say this: *there will be times when operating in this gift will require a heavier concentration for effective power.* The following illustrates how only those who shared an undeniable faith in Jesus's healing ministry were invited to participate. In the case of Jairus's daughter, Jesus would not allow anyone but Peter, James, and John to be with him. I believe the other disciples were not so confident and this work required only those who were unshakable in Jesus's ability to heal.

One of the synagogue officials named Jairus came up, and on seeing Him, fell at His feet and implored Him earnestly, saying, "My little daughter is at the point of death; please come and lay Your hands on her, so that she will get well and live."

Luke 8:41 (NKJV)

When He came into the house, He permitted no one to go in except Peter, James, and John, and the father and mother of the girl.

Luke 8:51 (NKJV)

Prayer and Fasting Is Essential

Prayer along with fasting increases our sensitivity to what God is up to and prepares us to carry out the assignment God has given us. Prayer is the quiet exhibition of our reliance on the Holy Spirit to empower us to lay hands on the sick. Prayer and fasting quickens us to be ready in season and out. James 5:14-15 (NKJV) says, "Is anyone among you sick? Let him call for the elders of the church, and let them pray over him, anointing him with oil in the name of the Lord. And the prayer of faith will save the sick, and the Lord will raise him up. And if he has committed sins, he will be forgiven." This passage speaks of preparedness. When an elder is called upon to pray for the sick, that elder had better be "prayed up." There is nothing more disheartening than for one of God's leaders to be unprepared or lack the faith to impact a life. Fasting in turn empties oneself of all the worldly impurities as the Holy Spirit gains greater control and releases an anointing to heal the sick and see them raised up.

When we fast, we must make sure our motives are right. We should not fast for selfish gain. Our hearts must be right when fasting. Fasting is for the purpose of spending more time doing spiritual things—and I am not talking about work. Fasting with prayer gets us synced with God. To be synced is to be in harmony with God for his healing process. Isaiah was addressing the Jews in Israel who were fasting with wrong motives. They wanted to look spiritual and draw attention to themselves. Look at God's counter response in Isaiah 58:8–12 (NASB).

The prophet reveals that when we fast with the right motive that our "light breaks forth like the morning." This means that you will begin to prosper in the newness of life (see verse 8). "If anyone is in Christ, he is a new creation" (2 Corinthians 5:17, NKJV)

I like this next one: He says that your healing "will spring forth speedily" (Isaiah 58:8, NASB). What the prophet is saying is that your past circumstances will be dealt with. When you pray and fast with the right motive and your heart is pure before the Lord and others, then your healing will come quickly.

Then if that's not enough, he says, "Your righteousness will go before you." (Isaiah 58:8, NASB). This is where your covenant agreement is connected to the divine and thus will result in peace and prosperity. Do you want God's peace and prosperity? Then choose to let God rule your heart and lean not on your own ways. Proverbs 3:3–6 (NKJV) says, "Trust in the LORD with all your heart, and lean not on your own understanding; In all your ways acknowledge Him, and He shall direct your paths."

And the prophet goes on to say, "The glory of the Lord will be your rear guard" (Isaiah 58:8, NASB). The splendor of God seen in the cloud and in the fire will be your ultimate protection. God will cause righteousness to lead you (in other words, allow you to prosper), and his glory will protect you from your past.

In verse 9, we see that God will respond favorably to our prayers when sin is renounced.

Other scriptures that speak to this issue are as follows:

- Psalm 66:18 (NKJV)—"If I regard wickedness in my heart, The Lord will not hear."

- Proverbs 28:9 (NKJV)—"He who turns away his ear from listening to the law, even his prayer is an abomination."
- Isaiah 65:24 (NKJV)—"It will also come to pass that before they call, I will answer; and while they are still speaking, I will hear."

Look at what else God will do. He says if we "remove the yoke, the pointing of the finger, and speaking wickedness" (Isaiah 58:9, NASB)—in other words, if we stop disrespecting others (like using the Roman technique of pointing the middle finger) and instead extend our soul to the hungry and take care of the afflicted—then the prophet says,

- "Then your light will rise in the darkness and your gloom will become like midday" (verse 10) Isaiah 58:10 (NASB)
- "And the Lord will continually guide you, and satisfy your desire in scorched places" (in drought) Isaiah 58:11 (NASB)
- "And give strength to your bones" (so that you can continue to press on, to make fat)Isaiah 58:11 (NASB)
- "And you will be like a watered garden" (nurtured, replenished, and sustained continually). Isaiah 58:11 (NASB)

- "And like a spring of water whose waters do not fail" Isaiah 58:11 (NASB)
- "Those from among you will rebuild the ancient ruins" (The remnant that remains God will use to restore, to usher in revival. I believe this time will be ushered in with fresh signs and wonders. There will be many healings nationally, physically, and spiritually. These all, I believe, are precursors to the return of Christ. This new season will unite the church and bring many to Jesus.) Isaiah 58:12 (NASB)
- "You will raise up the age-old foundations" Isaiah 58:12 (NASB)
- "And you will be called the repairer of the breach" (a time of great restoration) Isaiah 58:12 (NASB)
- "The restorer of the streets in which to dwell" (Isaiah 58:12). (Jerusalem will be established once again.)

Prayer and fasting is not only for leaders but also for the whole church. In Ephesians 6:18, Paul instructs the church of Ephesus to pray always: "praying always with all prayer and supplication in the Spirit, being watchful to this end with all perseverance and supplication for all the saints." All believers are to pray in the Spirit for the will of God. Notice this passage refers to "praying *always.*" Jesus communicated in Matthew 6:5, "when you pray," not *if* you pray. God is no respecter of persons.

All believers are to pray for healings. He wants all his children working and walking in their full anointing. Prayer and fasting are essential for the sensitivity necessary to discern how God is working so that one can be in tune with how he is working and how one is to participate. These are crucial times for our church and our nation. People throughout the world need a healing touch from our Lord. More than ever, the Lord is calling his people to come together in agreement to pray for our brothers in the faith, our community, and government.

Prayer promotes power of unity and agreement: "I tell you that if two of you on earth agree about anything you ask for, it will be done for you by my Father in heaven. For where two or three come together in my name, there am I with them" (Matthew 18:19–20, NIV).

Prayer exemplifies that we are part of the body of Christ: "So we, being many, are one body in Christ, and individually members of one another. Having then gifts differing according to the grace that is given to us, let us use them: if prophecy, let us prophesy in proportion to our faith" (Romans 12:5–6).

The majority of believers today have ceased praying and fasting. Others simply don't even participate in these spiritual exercises for lack of knowledge and understanding.

What Is Prayer?

Prayer is how we communicate to God on a daily basis. Praying should be like breathing, a natural process and an activity that we engage in all the time. Think about it! How can you say that you *love* someone if you don't talk to that person? Surely our vertical communication/ relationship with the Father through our Lord Jesus Christ will determine our horizontal relationship with others.

What Is Christian Fasting?

Biblically, fasting is abstaining from food, drink, sleep, or sex to focus on a period of spiritual growth. Specifically, we humbly deny the flesh of something to glorify God, enhance our spirit, and go deeper in our prayer life. If fasting were not important or biblical, Jesus would have never done this or spoken of it; however, he did: "Then Jesus, being filled with the Holy Spirit, returned from the Jordan and was led by the Spirit into the wilderness, being tempted for forty days by the devil. And in those days He ate nothing, and afterward, when they had ended, He was hungry"(Luke 4:2–3). Fasting is not used to make God do something that we want. Fasting is a spiritual weapon that will help us to control our flesh and allow the Holy Spirit to move through our lives. Fasting removes obstacles that hinder our walk with the Lord. It breaks bondages so we can attain breakthroughs. Fasting brings the power of God to our lives.

Here are a couple of fasts to consider:

- Absolutely no food or H2O (water). Only under extreme situations. (Acts 9:9)
- Normal or common fast: Fast only solid foods. (Luke 4:2)
- Partial fast (Daniel): Fast certain liquids or solid foods. (Daniel 1:2, 10:3)
- Supernatural fast: Fast water and food for forty days. (Exodus 24:15–18)

Here are two simple ways to prepare for a fast:

- Pray for direction and strength.
- Ask yourself the following questions:
- How many days and what type of fasting? Let the Holy Spirit guide you.
- When and how? Depending on the time and situation you may find some quiet time to pray. Take short walks and spend time with the Lord.

When fasting, consider the following:

- finding an appropriate time to pray
- replacing praying for the meal or the time spent eating
- taking a special time with the Lord (wake up earlier)
- praying whenever you think of food
- trying to plan in advance for a specific day
- having a list before you (i.e., what to pray for, scriptures, etc.)
- starting with praise and giving thanks to the Lord
- praying for your family, work (boss, coworkers, finances, etc.)
- praying for your church (pastor, leaders, children, youth, etc.)
- praying for direction

The most important thing is the intention of your heart and not the methods/styles and the duration of the fast. We are all in the process of growing and learning from this spiritual exercise that we are about to endure together.

Remember, he is our best food: "Then Jesus declared, 'I am the bread of life. He who comes to me will never go hungry, and he who believes in me will never be thirsty.'"

(John 6:35, NIV). We will never lack a good thing: "The lions may grow weak and hungry, but those who seek the Lord lack no good thing" (Psalm 34:10, NIV).

The Divine Order

In the body of Christ, the ecclesia, there is a means of operating in the spiritual gift of healing, and that is the church. These days, there are many who describe themselves as Christians, but don't see the value of the local church. I have seen my share of individuals who don't believe in apostolic authority. Dr. Martin Schmaltz, executive director of Apostolic Missions, has a global ministry in which he serves to empower born-again Christ followers to walk fully in the purposes for which God has created them. He gives this definition for Apostolic Authority:

Apostolic Authority is being sent by Jesus Christ with an authorization to use His inherent power to fulfill His purpose (Matthew 9:38, 10:16; Mark 3:14, 6:7; John 13:20). This apostolic sending has four parts:

- First, the source of authority comes from outside the one operating in authority.
- Second, authority has a specific area or place to operate.
- Third, there is usually a specific mission or purpose for the use of authority.
- Fourth and finally, it requires obedience and complete follow-through for authority to be effective.

Apostolic Authority is acting as Jesus' representative to this world to accomplish His purpose.

Jesus was sent by God to save the world (John 3:17), the Holy Spirit was sent to empower Christ followers (John 14:26, 15:26), and Christ followers are sent to carry out God's commands (John 20:21; 1 Corinthians 1:17). Too often, people have a bad experience in the church so they leave with the assumption that they have some greater knowledge or merit above scripture. They proudly believe they are God's man or woman, depart from underneath God's umbrella of protection, and fail to operate within God's divine order. You begin to understand Apostolic Authority when you understand what God has called you to do and respect the authority He has placed you under, over, or alongside of.

> Now you are the body of Christ, and members individually. And God has appointed these in the church: first apostles, second prophets, third teachers, after that miracles, then gifts of healings, helps, administrations, varieties of tongues.
>
> 1 Corinthians 12:27–28 (NKJV)

> And He Himself gave some to be apostles, some prophets, some evangelists, and some pastors and teachers, for the equipping of the saints for the work of ministry, for the edifying of the body of Christ, till we all come to the unity of the faith and of the knowledge of the Son of God, to a perfect man, to the measure of the stature of the fullness of Christ.
>
> Ephesians 4:11–13 (NKJV)

Now, 1 Corinthians 12:9 specifically addresses the spiritual gift of healing to accomplish his divine purposes.

Healing is also used in the *noun* form. The word here is *"therapeia"* (Greek). As stated earlier, Jesus the Christ is our healer; in addition, we will see that he is not only the source but also the object. In other words healing is *in* him—it is in his DNA; therefore, it is in *our* DNA. In other words, everything that we need for healing is found in Jesus the Christ, the anointed one of God. For example, if you were in need of an auto part for your Mercedes Benz, and the only place to get that part was through a Mercedes Benz parts distributor you wouldn't go to a Honda parts department or a Buick department for parts. You would be foolish and would waste a lot of time and money for something that would not work. Jesus Christ is the source and the object of healing. We must go to and through him for the power and induction of this divine action.

Healing, whether it is physical or spiritual, is not a game for God. He desires all who come to him to receive his touch. In Luke 9, we find Jesus healing all those who came after him. In the book of Revelation, we see a beautiful picture of the New Jerusalem and encamped therein is a "tree of life," whose leaves carried a cure to heal the nations. Ultimately, after this church age, in the new city, there will be no more sickness—physically or spiritually. You see, God loves the temple, because that is where he is worshiped. Our bodies are temples of the Holy Spirit (1 Corinthians 6:19); therefore, we must always live for him. God always exhibits his glory in his temple, and we are the temple of God.

While Jesus was on the earth, it was regularly his custom to communicate about the kingdom of God (over three hundred passages), and while he taught he would demonstrate what the kingdom of God was like as he healed many of his followers.

> But the crowds were aware of this and followed Him; and welcoming them, He began speaking to them about the kingdom of God and curing those who had need of healing.
>
> Luke 9:11 (NKJV)

In Revelation 22, the aged Apostle John is shown a beautiful reality of the healing virtue of the new Jerusalem. This passage depicts a tree straddling a river that had twelve different types of fruit (representing the twelve tribes), which blossomed each month (renewal). In other words, there was continual healing for the nations.

> Then he showed me a river of the water of life, clear as crystal, coming from the throne of God and of the Lamb, in the middle of its street. On either side of the river was the tree of life, bearing

twelve kinds of fruit, yielding its fruit every month; and the leaves of the tree were for the healing of the nations.

Revelation 22:1–2 (NKJV)

Bless the LORD, O my soul; and forget not all His benefits: who forgives all your iniquities, who heals all your diseases.

Psalm 103:2 (NKJV)

The Divine Process

Another word that helps to communicate healing is "iaomai" (Greek), which means to provide a physical treatment or cure. "Iama/Iasis" and "mapre" are the noun forms and are synonymous with a means of healing. The difference is that this application refers to a process, or the result of an act. This can trip up people of faith because they sometimes operate outside their boundaries and do not exercise a mature faith. Evangelical Christians oftentimes think because they declare it, it is supposed to happen at that moment. What we fail to see or ask is, what is God up to? Is he doing a work in my life to bring change? Is he developing my faith, my character? In other words, do we have enough faith to trust God in his process, to trust that he is up to something bigger than our immediate understanding? Do we see that we may be a part of his process (which may result in ultimate healing/separation from this life)? The bottom line is that this treatment or cure can be over a period of time, or it may happen immediately.

A recent revelation that came to me was the spiritual reality that God is always working. I have found many in Christian circles encouraging one another with the saying, "God is never late, never early, but always on time." This is very true. We must also understand that God is never on vacation. In other words, he never forgets you. You are always on his mind, and he is always working on your behalf. When God's children cry out to him, he hears; and when we ask for healing, he has already began a good work in us. Hear me clearly, when you do not see any movement when you pray (from your vantage point), know that God has not forgotten you. His divine process has already begun. You may not understand while you are going through it, but have faith in who God is and trust in what he is doing. David writes in Psalm 39 (NKJV) after going *through much pain and affliction*, "Lord, make me to know my end, and what is the measure of my days, that I may know how frail I am." He later writes in verse 7, "And now, Lord, what do I wait for? My hope is in You."

One weekend I was attending a pastor's retreat in Capon Springs, West Virginia. Before attending, the Holy Spirit began to speak to me, saying not to turn down open doors when invited to spend time with other senior-level ministers. As a church planter and under shepherd, I always felt the need to stay home, close to my church family (if you are a parent, I'm sure you can relate), but as my ministry grew in maturity, so did I. So while attending this retreat, I was invited to a conference in Denton, Texas, just outside of Dallas, and I immediately accepted the invitation. When I arrived at Dallas airport, Matt, a true Texan and cowboy, picked me up. Matt drove me to the Marriot Hotel where all the conference attendees were staying. The next morning, we were all shuttled to the Bridge Church where the main sessions were being held. During our ride, I began to sense in my spirit that there was something special about this brother, and soon enough the weekend would prevail. I was one of the last ones to go as I waited in the lobby, feeling a little disconnected. Then, a cowboy named Shaun (who was driving the van) looked at me sitting there, probably looking lost, and asked me if I was going to the conference and if I needed a ride.

Immediately, the spirit in this city boy from New Jersey began to connect with this Texas cowboy.

I truly enjoyed the conference, but was not sure why I was there. I continued to pray for the Holy Spirit to reveal to me why I was sent here. I soon found out that the answer was water—yes, water. My heart was drawn to mission work that was being done through a ministry called Water 10:42. The mission at the time was to dig a well in Kenya, Africa, where a group of people in the mountainous area had to travel more than four miles one way for water, and when the water arrived, it still was not sanitary. Then I found out that the two leaders of Water 10:42 were Matt and Shaun. Immediately, my heart overflowed with joy as I began to see why I was there. These two Texas brothers were not conference leaders, nor were they pastors—they were two men with a passion for water. I could hardly wait to get back to my Freedom Fellowship Church family to share with them what God was doing and present the opportunity we had to participate. Every year, we do a fundraiser for missions, but this one would be special. Over the next couple of months, my relationship with Matt and Shaun was strengthened, and our church was strengthened as well by their visit. In a short three-month period, we raised more than $12,000 for Water 10:42.

I, along with a team of leaders from my church, agreed that we would not send the check in the mail but travel to Denton and share in their joy as we gave them this gift for Water 10:42. Our trip was every thing we expected, but we would soon have greater revelation of why we were there. After rejoicing with the Matt, Shaun, Pastor Duane, and the Bridge Church family, we would find ourselves at the home of Matt's parents, Jody and Rhonda, and a host of guests.

Matt and Becky are the parents of two special twin girls, Madison and Makenzie. Makenzie was born with a life-threatening physical challenge; she was officially diagnosed with retina cancer on June 1, 2011. The doctors had located one large tumor in her left eye, causing blindness, as well as two smaller tumors in her right eye. Revelation of God's purpose and process is oftentimes progressive. That night, our team, which consisted of my wife Suzanne, Aaron, and his wife Tammy, and Tiffany and me found ourselves in a time of ministry where the Holy Spirit took charge, as prophetic words were being released over the people in that room. And one specific word that Suzanne received was that Makenzie would have victory over her cancerous tumor, but the family would go through a process. We were all confident believing God for a miracle. We knew at this time that our integration into this family's life was to be intercessors for them. This was bigger than all of us, and together, we would all stand by this family (I thank God that he gave Shaun to Matt, as a true friend and special brother in the Lord). Matt, Becky, and Makenzie would spend the next year with visits to specialists from Texas to Philadelphia, Pennsylvania, for chemo and radiation treatment. To God's glory and praise, Makenzie would be freed from cancer, but she would lose her eye. God led her to a specialist who gave her the most beautiful prosthetic eye (you could not tell the difference—shout out to the doctor!). Recently, I was able to visit with my Texas family and blessed to see Makenzie, who would soon be turning three years old, as rambunctious as any other child her age (if not more).

Here is Matt and Becky's story.

> As a parent, there is nothing I wouldn't do for my kids, but sometimes, life throws you a curve ball and puts you into positions that you have no control over. For myself, that is something very difficult to deal with, even when it comes to just day-to-day activities because I must confess, I am a bit of a control freak. Most of the time, I do what I can to attack the problem head-on, even if just to gain a little control over the situation,

but when it comes to something like your six-month-old child being diagnosed with cancer, there is not much control to gain.

When my wife and I decided it was time to start a family, we soon found out that we had a problem because as much as we tried and planned, it just didn't seem to work. Like others in our situation, we sought out help from the medical experts who, after numerous tests on both of us, could not find a reason we were unable to have a child.

We found ourselves, like many other couples, looking for help from a fertility clinic. After multiple tries and thousands of dollars, we finally got the news that we had long sought, we were pregnant. An announcement that a few short weeks later became a double blessing as we found out we were having twins. This came as a surprise to my wife and I as the doctor gave us a 25-percent chance of having just one child.

We should not have been shocked by the news because we had had multiple prophetic words spoken over us that this would happen. Months before, I was in Africa serving a local church; and on the day we were to return home, one of the pastors pulled me aside and told me that God had shown him a vision to share with me of four pink shoes in a hallway. While another word was given to us that we would have a double blessing of what we were praying for.

The day of double diapers, double feedings, double clothes, and twice as much lost sleep came on November 9, 2010. They girls arrived several weeks early, and my entire family was there to meet them. In fact, the nurses got on us for having so many visitors, but who was I to keep these gifts of God away from everyone? It took about a week for the girls to get stable enough for us to take them home, but once we did, I quickly realized I needed an instruction manual for being a father!

It was around month five when we began to notice something different with Kenzie's eye. The problem wasn't there all the time, and she had been to the doctor numerous times, and nothing was ever seen or diagnosed, so we thought we were just being overly protective parents. On Memorial Day 2011, Kenzie was lying in a bouncer chair directly under the living room light, and we noticed her left eye was hollow looking inside of her pupil. Something wasn't right.

We took her to the ER at Cook Children's hospital in Fort Worth to have it checked out.

They informed us that they could see something there but did not have the equipment to diagnose it any further. The next day, we were sent to a pediatric ophthalmologist who, after an examination, told us there was a problem with her retina, who then sent us to a retina specialist.

The following day, we were seen by the top retina specialist in the region. It was a day and diagnosis that would shake our world, our faith, and test my limits of being a father. The doctor told us that our daughter had bilateral retinoblastoma, a fancy medial term for saying she had cancer, in not just one, but both of her eyes. The priority at this point was not her sight, but preservation of life, as this type of cancer can spread to the brain very quickly and is very difficult to treat once that happens. The next day, we were at the oncology doctor putting a plan together to treat my six-month-old daughter with chemo, lasers, and cryo treatments. They also spent time giving us more information on what Kenzie was facing now and what she would face the rest of her life due to this type of cancer.

Retinoblastoma is from a defect in your DNA. Essentially, your body is lacking a gene it needs to naturally suppress cancer cells, and since the eyes are a quickly developing organ in the human body, they are a prime location for cancer to form during early development. In addition to this, they said she would have a 20–30 percent higher chance of getting any other form of cancer that one might get during his or her lifetime. They told us that she should be kept out of the sun as to avoid getting skin cancer and that she was almost guaranteed to pass it on to her children when that time came. Soon after this, we had our first EUA (exam under anesthesia) where the doctors would use lasers and cryo treatments on the cancer. It was at this time we got the news that her right eye had not one, but three separate tumors, with one of them pushing into the optic nerve. While her left eye had one massive tumor that had already destroyed the eye and caused the retina to detach and ultimately took her sight. It was the doctor's recommendation that her eye be removed in an effort to stop the spread of cancer to the brain, and that we should be prepared for Kenzie to have limited, if any, sight in her right eye.

The day of the eye removal is burned in my memory like it was yesterday. I can remember the last time I looked at Kenzie in both eyes right before I handed her over to the nurse. I lifted her up and told her I was sorry and felt like an utter failure as a father for not being able to protect her from this or take it away from her. I told her I wished it was me, knowing good and well she didn't understand a word I was saying.

The next twelve months was full of chemo treatments, hospital stays, and flights to Philadelphia to visit specialists, laser, and cryo treatments, and stress beyond belief. But it was also filled with circumstances that brought my family closer, chances to use this situation as an opportunity to share the Gospel, as well as faith-building times for my family and myself.

We began to pray for healing in Kenzie's body that the tumors would go away, that she would have perfect vision, that her DNA would be made new, and that she would be completely whole in Jesus's name. We were joined in this prayer by people around the world, by people we met in restaurants that wanted to pray for her and follow her story, by long lost friends, by people from countries across the ocean whom we had never met. It was if Kenzie's story took on a life of its own. The showing of support and prayer was overwhelming; it was proof positive that we are all one family in Christ.

After several treatments, the retina specialist was very positive in what was happening. The tumors in her right eye had stopped growing.

But as most doctors are, he was cautiously optimistic. As several more appointments came and went, her tumors began to die, turning into nothing more than scar tissue. Several positive things happened during this time. We found out that her hearing was 100 percent, even though it was at risk of being damaged during all the treatments, and we found out that Kenzie's vision in her right eye was right at 20/20. Even though she had had a tumor growing and placing pressure on her optic nerve, it had not affected her vision. We were also blessed during this time by an organization called Specs for Little Heroes that pays for the protective glasses that she must wear, which was a great financial blessing after all that we had been through.

During the middle of all this, the oncology department took a DNA sample from Kenzie, so that it could be studied, and they could locate the mutation in her DNA, in hopes to provide us with more information about what we could expect in the future. The test result took months to come back to us. The lady who called us about the results informed us that they could find no mutations in her DNA. She told us that she believed the results were a fluke and that she was ordering another test at a more in-depth level.

About a month later, I got a call from the same lady, who informed me that they could still not find any mutation in her DNA. She confessed to us that she had not seen this before in a patient with bilateral retinoblastoma and proceeded to tell us that she believed Kenzie should not have to worry about the increased risk of cancer, or about passing it on to her kids, and that she should live a normal life. She told me she could not explain it and neither could the retina specialist, or the oncologist, who insisted that it was there. Them being medical professionals, I can understand their hesitancy to say that it was a miracle, but as for my family and me, we knew. God had answered one of our biggest prayers during this whole process.

God is good and is ever faithful. My current prayer is that God will give my daughter a new eye so that she is truly 100 percent whole, and it will be my prayer until my dying breath. In my short time serving his kingdom, I have seen his miracles, a leg grow, AIDS cured, sicknesses removed, cancer disappear, lives saved, and one day soon, a new eye.

Here is the account of Kenzie's last doctor's visit.

> Kenzie had her end of the year EUA, and as we fully believed, it came back all clear. In addition, her MRI showed no growth of cancer in her orbits or head. The cyst that we found out about a few months ago, located behind her left eye implant, has remained stagnant and unchanged in size. This is a blessing as there is no need to remove it as it is not causing a problem with her implant or prosthetic. She continues to walk in perfect healing and health! Beginning in 2014, the doctors are cutting back the number of checkups and EUAs she will have due to the positive results we have been seeing over the past year. As always, we thank everyone for their prayers and support through this whole journey. You are all heroes to us!

The cool thing about Jesus is that he heals all the time. Sometimes, there was a process, and there were many times where he healed immediately. Here are a couple of cases where Jesus healed immediately. For instance, when the Gentile woman's daughter was healed:

Then Jesus said to her, "O woman, your faith is great; it shall be done for you as you wish." And her daughter was healed at once.

Matthew 15:28 (NKJV)
also Acts 9:34 (NKJV)

Then the man who was blind from birth:

Now as Jesus passed by, He saw a man who was blind from birth. And His disciples asked Him, saying, "Rabbi, who sinned, this man or his parents, that he was born blind?" Jesus answered, "Neither this man nor his parents sinned, but that the works of God should be revealed in him."

John 9:1–3 (NKJV)

Then there is the man lame from birth:

This man was listening to Paul as he spoke, who, when he had fixed his gaze on him and had seen that he had faith to be made well, said with a loud voice, "Stand upright on your feet." And he leaped up and began to walk.

Acts 14:9 (NASB)

And Publius's father was sick with fever and dysentery:

> And it happened that the father of Publius lay
> sick of a fever and dysentery. Paul went in to him
> and prayed, and he laid his hands on him and
> healed him. So when this was done, the rest of
> those on the island who had diseases also came
> and were healed.

Acts 28:8–10 (NKJV)

Luke used the word "healed" or "sōzō" fifteen times; the word means to save, to heal, to "make whole." His use in this context is that of a physician. The goal was to make the person whole (i.e., save the person from disease and its effects). The issue is that the people got too comfortable with Jesus. As Aesop's fable about the fox and lion tells us: "familiarity breeds contempt." Our Lord's long residence in Nazareth merely as a townsman had made him *too common*, incapacitating the people from appreciating him as others did who were *less familiar with his everyday demeanor in private life.* This is a most important principle, to which the wise will pay due regard.[5]

> And He said to them, "No doubt you will quote
> this proverb to Me, 'Physician, heal yourself!

Whatever we heard was done at Capernaum, do here in your hometown as well.'"

Luke 4:23 (NASB)

Those who had seen it reported to them how the man who was demon-possessed had been made well.

Luke 8:36 (NASB)

And He said to them, "Go and tell that fox, 'Behold, I cast out demons and perform cures today and tomorrow, and the third day I reach My goal.'"

Luke 13:32 (NASB)

For she was saying to herself, "If I only touch His garment, I will get well." But Jesus turning and seeing her said, "Daughter, take courage; your faith has made you well." At once the woman was made well.

Matthew 9:21–22, (NASB),
see Acts 4:9, NASB)

Jesus was going through all the cities and villages, teaching in their synagogues and proclaiming the gospel of the kingdom, and healing every kind of disease and every kind of sickness. Seeing the people, *He felt compassion for them, because they were distressed and dispirited like sheep without a shepherd. Then He said to His disciples,* "The harvest is plentiful, but the workers are few. Therefore beseech the Lord of the harvest to send out workers into His harvest."

Matthew 9:35–38 (NASB)

Naaman, the commander of the army of the king of Syria, was not only a great commander who had won many victories for the Lord, but he was known to be an honorable and well-respected man. However, Naaman had one problem: he was a leper. During one of his raids, a young girl was taken captive, and she became a servant in Naaman's house. God used this servant girl in this great commander's life for healing. She told him to go see Elisha, who was a prophet in Samaria. After many attempts to use his political power, he eventually agreed to some less conventional instructions for his healing. Elisha the prophet told him to go down to the dirty Jordan River and dip seven times. Actually, the Scriptures say, "Go and wash in the Jordan seven times, and your flesh shall be restored to you, and you shall be clean" (2 Kings 5:14–17, NKJV); (Luke 4:27, NKJV). In other words, the dirt of the Jordan River would be a scrub bath. This seemed to be a very humiliating process for a commander, but he exercised his faith in God's process and was healed.

Jesus Christ our Lord was having an exchange with Thomas and Philip (John 14:1–14, NKJV). Many of the other disciples were there, but these two became concerned about Jesus leaving. They had put their trust in him and had seen him perform many great signs and wonders. Jesus's word of comfort was consistent: "Believe Me" (John 14:11, NKJV).

> Most assuredly, I say to you, he who believes in Me, the works that I do he will do also; and greater works than these he will do, because I go to My Father. And whatever you ask in My name, that I will do, that the Father may be glorified in the Son. If you ask anything in My name, I will do it.
>
> John 14:12–14

National Healing

The Old Testament usage, "to heal" is mostly used in the context of "healing of the nation," which is performed through repentance and restoration of God's holy people. The most familiar passage to see this illustrated is 2 Chronicles 7:14 (NKJV), "If My people who are called by My name will humble themselves, and pray and seek My face, and turn from their wicked ways, then I will hear from heaven, and will forgive their sin and heal their land." This is what God says he will do when we turn our hearts back to him. This passage is not exclusive to Israel; God wants all his created beings, all of humanity to know him and to turn to him for life's sustenance.

Repentance Required

National healing begins with the change of heart by large groups of people. This starts with an individual but doesn't stay there. National healing is permeated through the individual, the head of a family, a community leader, a statesman, a congressional leader, a president to include leaders of people on a national scale. Healing on this national scale is not limited to race or ethnicity or social or economic status. It is God's will that people everywhere should repent and turn to him.

The Prophet Isaiah says,

> For the heart of this people has become dull, With their ears they scarcely hear, And they have closed their eyes, Otherwise they would see with their eyes, Hear with their ears, And understand with their heart and return, And I would heal them.

Matthew 13:15 (NKJV),
John 12:40 (NKJV), Isaiah 58:8 (NASB)

This turning to God requires a change of heart and direction. The Apostle Paul reminds us in Romans 3:23 that "all have sinned and come short of the glory of God." Later, in Romans 5:8 (NKJV), we read, "But God demonstrates His own love toward us, in that while we were still sinners, Christ died for us." So if we rid ourselves of human pride and trust the finished work of Jesus's death and resurrection, then we can be restored and receive the gift of salvation—all because of Jesus Christ our Lord. "For the wages of sin is death, but the gift of God is eternal life in Christ Jesus our Lord" (Romans 6:23, NKJV).

King Zedekiah was a wicked king who reigned over Judah and Jerusalem (2 Chronicles 36:11). He was actually a rebel; he didn't want to listen to anyone. On numerous occasions during his twenty-one-year reign, Jeremiah the prophet would prophesize that God's judgment was coming, and if Zedekiah put his trust in God for the care of his people, God would deliver him. Zedekiah continued to harden his heart, so God eventually gave him and his descendants over to Babylonian captivity. Zedekiah's life would end by witnessing the slaughter of all his sons before his very eyes, then having his eyes being plucked out and locked in a prison until he died. "Then he blinded the eyes of Zedekiah; and the king of Babylon bound him with bronze fetters and brought him to Babylon and put him in prison until the day of his death" (Jeremiah 52:11, NASB). This is a tragic ending because he chose not to turn from his wicked ways, repent, and turn to God.

God loves us, and by his sovereignty, he loves to restore his people. In Hosea 6:1 (NKJV), the prophet says, "Come, and let us return to the LORD; for He has torn, but He will heal us; He has stricken, but He will bind us up." God will do whatever it takes to bring us back to him. He does not release this act of healing by dealing with symptoms, but the root issues. When God begins to turn our world upside down to the point of breaking us into many pieces, we should know that he can put our lives back together for his glory. Turning back to God begins with humbling ourselves and then turning back to him. This is repentance! When our ascents of tears are upward to our great God and King, then national healing is released.

> Oh LORD my God, I cried out to You, and You healed me.
>
> Psalm 30:2 (NKJV)

Forgiveness Required

The road to God's healing for the nation must include forgiveness. I believe we are in a season where God is calling his people across the globe to learn to walk in mercy and compassion by forgiving and being forgiven. This is the pathway to emotional healing. God makes healing through forgiveness possible, and he has initiated this forgiveness through his Son Jesus's death on the cross.

> The Spirit of the Lord is upon Me, Because He anointed Me to preach the gospel to the poor. He has sent Me to proclaim release to the captives, And recovery of sight to the blind, To set free those who are oppressed, To proclaim the favorable year of the Lord.
>
> Luke 4:18 (NKJV)

To understanding healing through forgiveness is critical for national healing because great relationships are forged together on the basis of love and forgiveness. The truth about forgiveness isn't easy because you never have to forgive someone for something that doesn't matter to you. You don't have to forgive someone for helping you, making you smile, or making you feel good. The only time you have to forgive is when you've been hurt by someone. I was recently speaking with my wife, and she was telling me that emotional healing is a process. She says, "It's like walking around with a big gaping wound." Sometimes, these wounds take months, sometimes even years, for healing. She had to learn to give the people and her pain over to God, and if you don't learn to do this, you will become bitter. Emotional pain can lead to physical ailments. There is the tensing of heart as well as unrest in the mind. The pathway to this emotional healing is forgiveness.

The good news about forgiveness is that it keeps Satan from gaining a foothold on your relationships. Paul tells us this in the New Testament. Read this out loud, please:

> The focus of my letter wasn't on punishing the offender but on getting you to take responsibility for the health of the church. So if you forgive him, I forgive him. Don't think I'm carrying around a list of personal grudges. The fact is that I'm joining in with your forgiveness, as Christ is with us, guiding us. After all, we don't want to unwittingly give Satan an opening for yet more mischief—we're not oblivious to his sly ways!
>
> 2 Corinthians 2:10–11 (MSG)

Have you ever known anyone who was so consumed by anger or hate that they couldn't think rationally? It happens all the time! When we're consumed by hatred or even consumed by our hurt, Satan can outwit us. Forgiveness it is a topic that should be covered over and over again. Why? Because our efforts to pursue truth and self-justification lie underneath our age-old jealousies, petty agendas, strife, and sheer humanness that affects us all. Forgiving others who have hurt us can be a difficult task, and in my opinion, the dangerous "seed" that we often mix with an unforgiving spirit is pride. This is a very sensitive issue for me because not only do I have to work this out in my own life, but I carry the burden for each of you to walk in forgiveness as well. We need national forgiveness. We need to see ethnic groups across the human spectrum unencumbered by hatred that induces physical and emotional damage.

Psychologist Michelle Nelson says there are three degrees, or types of forgiveness:

1. *Detached forgiveness*—there is a reduction of negative feelings toward the offender, but no reconciliation takes place.
2. *Limited forgiveness*—there is a reduction in negative feelings toward the offender, and the relationship is partially restored though there is a decrease in the emotional intensity of the relationship.
3. *Full forgiveness*—there is a total termination of negative feelings toward the offender, and the relationship is fully restored.

Because Jesus knew that this topic of forgiveness was so important, he devoted an entire parable about it. Matthew 18:21–35 chronicles the parable of the unmerciful servant.

Here are ten observations to take away from this encounter.

1. The first observation is the number Jesus uses for the number of times we must forgive.

   Peter wants to know how high to count; Jesus doesn't like it when we keep score.

   The Jews of that day taught that you could forgive a brother as many as three times for an offense, but after the fourth time, there was no forgiveness. Peter knows Jesus's heart of compassion, so he doubles the number and adds one. "Is seven times enough, Lord?" he asks.

   Jesus tells him, "Seventy times seven." It's an allusion to a statement by Lamech in the book of Genesis that Lamech would take vengeance not seven times on someone who had wronged him, but seventy-seven times. Since no one can keep count for that long, it might as well be an unlimited number. When it comes to forgiveness, Jesus doesn't want us to keep score; he just wants us to forgive.

2. Here's the second observation. The Greek word for forgiveness is "aphiēmi" (afa-me), which means to completely cancel, to put aside your anger, pride, grievances, and your need to be right.

   It is interesting Peter is having this dialogue with the Lord Jesus Christ. Peter, whose name means "petros" (little rock), would learn a deeper meaning of what it is to forgive. Jesus told Peter not seven times, but seventy times seven. You might ask the question, how? Only through a surrendered life to Christ can the Holy Spirit enable you to forgive. You want to change the world? Then learn how to forgive completely.

> What impresses the world most is changed lives for which there is no natural explanation.
>
> —RT Kendall

"aphiēmi"—to set aside your anger, pride, grievances, and your need to be right.[1]

> Do not let any unwholesome talk come out of your mouths, but only what is helpful for building others up according to their needs, that it may benefit those who listen. And do not grieve the Holy Spirit of God, with whom you were sealed for the day of redemption. Get rid of all bitterness, rage and anger, brawling and slander, along with every form of malice. Be kind and compassionate to one another, forgiving each other, just as in Christ God forgave you.
>
> Ephesians 4:29–32 (NIV)

3. A talent equals fifteen years of wages. This is a big sum!

---

[1] Strong, J. (2009). *A Concise Dictionary of the Words in the Greek Testament and The Hebrew Bible*. Bellingham, WA: Logos Bible Software.

4. A denarius equals one day's wage. In those days, a denarius was equal to about twenty dollars.

5. The servant owed an outrageous amount to his master. Fifteen years' wages times ten thousand equals one hundred and fifty thousand years' worth of debt. Actually, the ten thousand talents equal about ten million dollars!

6. No one borrows one hundred and fifty thousand years' worth of pay. This servant must have been an embezzler.

7. The king is willing to cancel an inconceivably large debt—one that in no way could be repaid.

   The sad news is that the servant *is not* willing to cancel a debt owed to him. As I said earlier, a denarius was a single day's wage for a soldier or laborer. So the debt owed to the servant was about one hundred days' worth of pay—that comes to about $2,000. After being forgiven an astronomical amount, the servant isn't willing to set aside his anger over a smaller amount.

8. The king is much more angry about the servant's lack of "aphiēmi" (afa-me) for a fellow servant than about his sin against the king.

   Jesus is saying, "God may be upset when you sin against Him, but He is angry when you refuse to forgive a friend."

9. How we treat others matters to God just as much as it matters of how we treat him. God's people/nation wide must walk in forgiveness and turn to him.

10. And my favorite, *those who have been forgiven must forgive.*

This is why Jesus, in the Lord's Prayer, instructs us to say, "And forgive us our debts as we forgive our debtors."

When Peter wants to know how many times we should forgive someone, Jesus tells him this story to help him see the heart of the Father. The Holy Spirit also wants to reveal to us that Satan is the cunning embezzler who wants you to believe that you cannot not be forgiven, nor is it possible for you to forgive others. When Jesus mentioned the size of the debt to his first century listeners, every one of them expected to hear that this man would be thrown into prison, or worse. And that starts to happen to him until he asks for patience (mercy).

When the servant asks for mercy, the king sets aside his anger and not only grants his request, he goes one better. Instead of giving him time to pay back the debt of ten million dollars, which he could never do, the king cancels the debt; he forgives him.

But when this recipient of great forgiveness is asked to grant more time to someone with a small debt, he throws him in prison. This, the king cannot stand. He actually gets angry and has the man not only thrown into prison, but also tortured for his sins.

Have you ever been in a position where you wanted someone to forgive you but were afraid they wouldn't? Probably some of you are in this position today. I've been there! If you were to add up all the things I have done

Kurt W. Wallace

to hurt the Lord or embezzled from his glory, my debt would be huge—limitless (at least one hundred and fifty thousand years' worth)!

> If we confess our sins, He is faithful and just to forgive us our sins and to cleanse us from all unrighteousness. If we say that we have not sinned, we make Him a liar, and His word is not in us.
>
> 1 John 1:9–10 (NKJV)

When I daily ask God to forgive me, he does so because of his great mercy, not because I deserve it. Thank God, he cancels my debt.

So why should nations forgive? I'm going to give you four reasons.

1. Satan. I don't know about you, but I do not want to give him a foothold in my life. When I harbor anger against a friend that gives him a weak spot where he can come in and drill deep into me, I don't want him anywhere near my life. So I want to forgive.
2. And then, there is…*me* or ourselves. I want peace in my life, not bitterness. When I refuse to forgive someone, I suffer far more than they do.

    The truth is, when you refuse to forgive someone, they own you. You hesitate to go anywhere where you

126

might encounter them. Your blood pressure goes up every time you think about them. The reason we don't want to forgive is because we want to hurt the other person, when the reality is we hurt ourselves far more by our refusal.

3. You and I are not perfect. Compared to the person who's offended you, their debt might be one hundred and fifty thousand years, but yours is at least one hundred days, isn't it?

    If you could stand in one of two lines—one for those who need no forgiveness because they've never hurt anybody, wronged anybody, wounded anybody and one for those who have hurt others—which line would you stand in? On the national stage, what line would America stand in?

    We all need forgiveness, so we all should want to be forgiven. How can we withhold from someone else that which we hope to be given by someone else? Though the points above are directed to individuals, as a nation, America should likewise model forgiveness to other nations of the world because we have been given so much.

4. And the last reason why we should forgive is this: Christ forgave you, me—*us*!

    The Bible says that the last thing Jesus said while He was dying on the Cross was, "It is finished." That phrase is just one word in Greek: "tetelestai" (tet-a-lest-a). The word means, "paid in full." If a Greek merchant writes that across the bottom of your bill, you owe no more debt.

Have you ever paid off a big bill or balance that you have been paying on for a long time? When it is finally paid in full, how good that feels! But in this case, we have done nothing, and Christ has paid it all.

Jesus knew what he was going to do when He told the disciples this parable. He knew he was going to be the one to forgive the debt we couldn't hope to pay by paying it himself—"tetelestai" (tet-a-lest-a), *paid in full*.

You might say, "You don't know what that group of people did to me!" Well, Jesus does. And someday, he'll right all wrongs. Meanwhile, he wants you to live at peace.

"But you don't know what my country did to me!" Jesus does. And someday, he'll right all wrongs. Meanwhile, he wants you to live at peace.

So then, how do I forgive?

How Do I Forgive?

1. Make a decision to forgive. If you wait until you *feel* like forgiving, you'll never get there. Being hurt is an emotional event and emotions don't heal by themselves. They heal with the help of your will. First, make a decision to forgive. Later, your feelings will follow.
2. Say the words—at least to yourself. When I say these words in my mind—"I forgive you," "I forgive my country,"

"I forgive..."—there is something tangible that happens in my heart when I release someone from the wrong they have done to me. It starts with my will, so even if you don't feel like it, once you make the decision, say to yourself, "I forgive..." Your feelings will follow. The best kind of forgiveness forgives and then allows the past to stay in the past. It's time to move forward!

3. When you forgive, you forgive.

"Aphiēmi" (afa-me) means put your anger, your hurt, your resentment, and your right to revenge aside because this is where wars are started. Don't use the occasion as an opportunity to reopen an old wound, restart a previous war, or score points by appearing superior because you were the one who was big enough to forgive first. Some of our frustrations stem from the fact that we think we know a better way, or we don't like how something is done so we become bitter (which is actually the source of pride).

When there is a need to confront, confront. But when your purpose is to forgive, don't cast blame, bring up old issues, try to score points, or set yourself up to win the next round. When you forgive, *forgive*.

4. Forgive completely!

Watch this for a minute. In Colossians 3:13, the Apostle Paul says *forgive as the lord forgave you.*

Forgive *as* the Lord forgave you. What types of words could be substituted for that little word "as" right there?

How about "just like"?

How about "in the same way"?

Forgive just like Jesus forgave. How did Jesus forgive?

Jesus forgave fully, willingly, humbly, unconditionally, before we ever knew we needed forgiveness; Jesus laid aside his anger and forgave.

In the Lord's Prayer, Jesus teaches us to pray by saying, "And forgive us our debts as we forgive our debtors" (Matthew 5:13, NKJV).

Look, I've done some embarrassing things in my life. I've done some stupid things in my life. You've read my story earlier in this book, but more devastating is the fact that I have also done many hurtful things, some of them deliberately. Yet when I asked God to forgive me, the Bible says in Psalm 103:12 (NKJV), "As far as the east is from the west, so far has He removed our transgressions from us." How far is that? The bottom line is that God wants us to be forgivers and to walk in forgiveness. This is quintessential to our healing as a people and a nation.

5. Forgive Repeatedly

So I forgive, and then something else comes up—something that reminds me of what that person did—and I get mad again. So now what do I do? I forgive again. If it's a fresh wound, I may have to forgive five or six times a day. If it's an older wound, I might find myself having feelings I need to set aside every few weeks or maybe every few years. When you forgive, realize that you may have to forgive the same offense more than once—not because the offense needs to be forgiven multiple times, but because you need to set aside your anger multiple times.

6. Forgiveness does not mean forgetting.

When someone hurts you deeply, your brain records that. It's there and you can't forget it. My wife will tell you that she oftentimes forgets where she puts things, but she can remember every detail about something I did or said to her. She can go back years! Go figure! So forgiveness does not mean forgetting, you just "aphiēmi" (afa-me) or lay it aside.

7. In the same vein, forgiveness doesn't mean trusting. Here's an important distinction:

Forgiveness must be granted; it can't be earned.

Trust can't be granted. It must be earned.

You've heard the saying, "Fool me once, shame on you. Fool me twice, shame on me."

When an individual or even a nation establishes a pattern of untrustworthy behavior, you can't trust them. It wouldn't make sense. So when an offense is repeated and forgiveness is sought, we must grant forgiveness. And if the offending party wants to be restored, then you set up a system by which they can prove that they really have changed.

If I am the offending party, I need to change my behavior because I want you to be able to trust me, and I know you can't unless I prove myself trustworthy.

This is very important. Forgiveness must be granted; no one can earn it. Trust must be earned, granting it would do no one any favors.

Again, national healing is a work of God. When we turn our hearts back to him, he will restore. This begins with repentance and forgiveness individually and collectively. God has promised that he will heal our land, if we "humble [ourselves], and pray and seek [His] face, and turn from [our] wicked ways." Lord, please heal our nation.

"Blessed is the nation whose God is the Lord,
The people He has chosen as His own inheritance."

Psalm 33:12 (NKJV)

Conclusion

God loves us, and he does not allow anything to cause his children pain without cause. He is our healer as is his Son. God loves to heal and so does Jesus. To truly understand healing is to ask God what he is up to. Then, you can begin to walk with and participate with God on the journey.

It is also important to understand that because we live in a fallen world we are susceptible to injury and disease. The spiritual realty is that every one will face death at some point in time. For those who have trusted Jesus Christ as Lord and Savior, the great mystery of hope is that one day, we will all walk in ultimate healing and spend eternity with our Lord in heaven. The bodies we have will be done away with, and we will have new bodies fit for our new home.

For those who deny the Lord in this life, there is no hope, and the future is filled with darkness and separation from the blessedness of our Lord and Savior, Jesus Christ.

God's love is not limited to some; he loves everyone no matter your state. It is his desire that all come to know his Son and receive him as Lord. So we can conclude that it is God's desire that all humanity embrace spiritual, physical, and national healing. This begins with repentance, which requires action on every level. If God is love, then we too should respond to his love.

We demonstrate God's love by hearing and obeying his word, and loving others. God's people commit themselves to grow in an abiding relationship with God through his Son Jesus Christ and the indwelling person of the Holy Spirit. This abiding relationship is not "name it and claim it," but a yielding with a desire to know God, and the only way to know God is to know his Son and trusting the Holy Spirit's teaching and leading. Doing so ignites an inward change in the believer, allowing for forgiveness that glorifies God.

I pray that this book has in some way drawn your heart closer to God. It has been a blessing to me as I walk my journey with him. I am praising God every day for his healing mercy on my life. My bone cancer came back with a negative report, and I know it is the work of God on my life. This sickness has made me reflect on the mercies of our Lord and has deepened my faith by revealing my doubts. Tomorrow is not promised, so let us make every day count for our great God and King Jesus.

> Many, O LORD my God, are Your wonderful works which You have done; and Your thoughts toward us cannot be recounted to You in order; It I would declare and speak of them they are more than can be numbered.
>
> Psalm 40:5(NKJV)

Appendix

Healing Scriptures

"So Abraham prayed to God; and God healed Abimelech, his wife, and his female servants. Then they bore children." Genesis 20:17 (NKJV).

"If men contend with each other, and one strikes the other with a stone or with his fist, and he does not die but is confined to his bed, if he rises again and walks about outside with his staff, then he who struck him shall be acquitted. He shall only pay for the loss of his time, and shall provide for him to be thoroughly healed." Exodus 21:18–19 (NKJV)

"If the body develops a boil in the skin, and it is healed." Leviticus 13:18 (NKJV), (See verses 18–27.)

"But if the bright spot stays in one place, *and* has not spread on the skin, but has faded, it *is* a swelling from the burn. The priest shall pronounce him clean, for it *is* the scar from the burn." Leviticus 13:28 (NKJV), (See verses 28–37.)

"If a man or a woman has bright spots on the skin of the body, *specifically* white bright spots." Leviticus 13:38 (NKJV), (See verses 38–46.)

"So Moses took the rod from before the Lord as He commanded him. And Moses and Aaron gathered the assembly together before the rock; and he said to them, 'Hear now, you rebels! Must we bring water for you out of this rock?' Then Moses lifted his hand and struck the rock twice with his rod; and water came out abundantly, and the congregation and their animals drank. Then the Lord spoke to Moses and Aaron, 'Because you did not believe Me, to hallow Me in the eyes of the children of Israel, therefore you shall not bring this assembly into the land which I have given them.'" Numbers 20:9–12 (NKJV)

"The Lord will strike you with the boils of Egypt, with tumors, with the scab, and with the itch, from which you cannot be healed." Deuteronomy 28:27 (NKJV)

"The LORD will strike you in the knees and on the legs with severe boils which cannot be healed, and from the sole of your foot to the top of your head." Deuteronomy 28:35 (NKJV)

"So it was, when they had finished circumcising all the people, that they stayed in their places in the camp till they were healed." Joshua 5:8 (NKJV)

"So they said, "If you send away the ark of the God of Israel, do not send it empty; but by all means return it to Him with a trespass offering. Then you will be healed, and it will be known to you why His hand is not removed from you." 1 Samuel 6:3 (NKJV)

"Then he went out to the source of the water, and cast in the salt there, and said, 'Thus says the LORD: 'I have healed this water; from it there shall be no more death or barrenness.' So the water remains healed to this day, according to the word of Elisha which he spoke.'" 2 Kings 2:21–22 (NKJV)

"So he went down and dipped seven times in the Jordan, according to the saying of the man of God; and his flesh was restored like the flesh of a little child, and he was clean." 2 Kings 5:14 (NKJV)

"Return and tell Hezekiah the leader of My people, 'Thus says the LORD, the God of David your father: "I have heard your prayer, I have seen your tears; surely I will heal you. On the third day you shall go up to the house of the LORD." 2 Kings 20:5 (NKJV)

"If My people who are called by My name will humble themselves, and pray and seek My face, and turn from their wicked ways, then I will hear from heaven, and will forgive their sin and heal their land." 2 Chronicles 7:14 (NKJV)

"And in the thirty-ninth year of his reign, Asa became diseased in his feet, and his malady was severe; yet in his disease he did not seek the LORD, but the physicians." 2 Chronicles 16:12 (NKJV)

"And the LORD listened to Hezekiah and healed the people." 2 Chronicles 30:20 (NKJV)

"But they mocked the messengers of God, despised His words, and scoffed at His prophets, until the wrath of the LORD arose against His people, till there was no remedy." 2 Chronicles 36:16 (NKJV)

"Have mercy on me, O LORD, for I am weak; O LORD, heal me, for my bones are troubled." Psalm 6:2 (NKJV)

"O LORD my God, I cried out to You, and You healed me." Psalm 30:2 (NKJV)

"I said, "LORD, be merciful to me; heal my soul, for I have sinned against You." Psalm 41:4 (NKJV)

"Bless the LORD, O my soul; and all that is within me, bless His holy name! Bless the LORD, O my soul, and forget not all His benefits: Who forgives all your iniquities, who heals all your diseases Psalm 103:1–3 (NKJV)

"He sent His word and healed them, and delivered them from their destructions." Psalm 107:20 (NKJV)

"He heals the brokenhearted and binds up their wounds." Psalm 147:3 (NKJV)

"A sound heart is life to the body, but envy is rottenness to the bones." Proverbs 14:30 (NKJV)

"A merry heart does good, *like* medicine, but a broken spirit dries the bones." Proverbs 17:22 (NKJV)

"A time to kill, and a time to heal; a time to break down, and a time to build up." Ecclesiastes 3:3 (NKJV)

"Make the heart of this people dull, and their ears heavy, and shut their eyes; Lest they see with their eyes, and hear with their ears, and understand with their heart, and return and be healed." Isaiah 6:10 (NKJV)

"Moreover the light of the moon will be as the light of the sun, and the light of the sun will be sevenfold, as the light of seven days, in the day that the LORD binds up the bruise of His people and heals the stroke of their wound." Isaiah 30:26 (NKJV)

"But He was wounded for our transgressions, He was bruised for our iniquities; the chastisement for our peace was upon Him, And by His stripes we are healed." Isaiah 53:5 (NKJV)

"I have seen his ways, and will heal him; I will also lead him, and restore comforts to him and to his mourners." Isaiah 57:18 (NKJV)

"Then your light shall break forth like the morning, your healing shall spring forth speedily, and your righteousness shall go before you; the glory of the LORD shall be your rear guard." Isaiah 58:8 (NKJV)

"The Spirit of the Lord GOD is upon Me, because the LORD has anointed Me to preach good tidings to the poor; He has sent Me to heal the brokenhearted, to proclaim liberty to the captives, and the opening of the prison to those who are bound;" Isaiah 61:1 (NKJV); (see Luke 4:18)

"Return, you backsliding children, *and* I will heal your backslidings." "Indeed we do come to You, for You are the LORD our God." Jeremiah 3:22 (NKJV)

"They have also healed the hurt of My people slightly, Saying, 'Peace, peace!' When there is no peace." Jeremiah 6:14 (NKJV)

"For they have healed the hurt of the daughter of My people slightly, saying, 'Peace, peace!' When there is no peace." Jeremiah 8:11 (NKJV)

"We looked for peace, but no good came; And for a time of health, and there was trouble!" Jeremiah 8:15 (NKJV)

"Have You utterly rejected Judah? Has Your soul loathed Zion? Why have You stricken us so that there is no healing for us? We looked for peace, but there was no good; And for the time of healing, and there was trouble." Jeremiah 14:19 9 (NKJV)

"Heal me, O Lord, and I shall be healed; Save me, and I shall be saved, for You are my praise." Jeremiah 17:14 (NKJV)

"There is no one to plead your cause, that you may be bound up; You have no healing medicines." Jeremiah 30:13 (NKJV)

"'For I will restore health to you and heal you of your wounds,' says the Lord, 'because they called you an outcast saying, "This is Zion; No one seeks her."'" Jeremiah 30:17 (NKJV)

"Behold, I will bring it health and healing; I will heal them and reveal to them the abundance of peace and truth." Jeremiah 33:6 (NKJV)

"Babylon has suddenly fallen and been destroyed. Wail for her! Take balm for her pain; perhaps she may be healed. We would have healed Babylon, But she is not healed. Forsake her, and let us go everyone to his own country; For her judgment reaches to heaven and is lifted up to the skies." Jeremiah 51:8–9 (NKJV)

"The weak you have not strengthened, nor have you healed those who were sick, nor bound up the broken, nor brought back what was driven away, nor sought what was lost; but with force and cruelty you have ruled them. So they were scattered because there was no shepherd; and they became food for all the beasts of the field when they were scattered." Ezekiel 34:4–5 (NKJV)

"Then he said to me: 'This water flows toward the eastern region, goes down into the valley, and enters the sea. When it reaches the sea, its waters are healed. And it shall be that every living thing that moves, wherever the rivers go, will live. There will be a very great multitude of fish, because these waters go there; for they will be

healed, and everything will live wherever the river goes.'"
Ezekiel 47:8–9 (NKJV)

"Come, and let us return to the LORD; For He has torn,
but He will heal us; He has stricken, but He will bind us
up." Hosea 6:1 (NKJV)

"When I would have healed Israel, Then the iniquity
of Ephraim was uncovered, And the wickedness of
Samaria. For they have committed fraud; a thief comes
in; A band of robbers takes spoil outside." Hosea 7:1
(NKJV)

"I taught Ephraim to walk, taking them by their arms;
but they did not know that I healed them." Hosea 11:3
(NKJV)

"Your injury has no healing, your wound is severe. All
who hear news of you will clap their hands over you, for
upon whom has not your wickedness passed continually?"
Nahum 3:19 (NKJV)

"But to you who fear My name The Sun of Righteousness
shall arise with healing in His wings; and you shall go
out and grow fat like stall-fed calves." Malachi 4:2 (NKJV)

"And Jesus went about all Galilee, teaching in their synagogues, preaching the gospel of the kingdom, and healing all kinds of sickness and all kinds of disease among the people. 24 Then His fame went throughout all Syria; and they brought to Him all sick people who were afflicted with various diseases and torments, and those who were demon-possessed, epileptics, and paralytics; and He healed them." Matthew 4:23–24 (NKJV), (also see Mark 1:39, Luke 4:40–44)

"The centurion answered and said, 'Lord, I am not worthy that You should come under my roof. But only speak a word, and my servant will be healed.'" Matthew 8:8 (NKJV), also Luke 7:1–10 (NKJV)

"When evening had come, they brought to Him many who were demon-possessed. And He cast out the spirits with a word, and healed all who were sick, that it might be fulfilled which was spoken by Isaiah the prophet, saying: 'He Himself took our infirmities And bore our sicknesses.'" Matthew 8:16–17 (NKJV); (also see Mark 1:29–34, Luke 4:38–41)

"While He spoke these things to them, behold, a ruler came and worshiped Him, saying, 'My daughter has just died, but come and lay Your hand on her and she will live.'" Matthew 9:18 (NKJV)

"And suddenly, a woman who had a flow of blood for twelve years came from behind and touched the hem of His garment. For she said to herself, 'If only I may touch His garment, I shall be made well.' But Jesus turned around, and when He saw her He said, 'Be of good cheer, daughter; your faith has made you well.' And the woman was made well from that hour." Matthew 9:20–22 (NKJV)

"When Jesus came into the ruler's house, and saw the flute players and the noisy crowd wailing, He said to them, 'Make room, for the girl is not dead, but sleeping.' And they ridiculed Him. But when the crowd was put outside, He went in and took her by the hand, and the girl arose. And the report of this went out into all that land." Matthew 9:23–26 (NKJV)

"When Jesus departed from there, two blind men followed Him, crying out and saying, 'Son of David, have mercy on us!' And when He had come into the house, the blind men came to Him. And Jesus said to them, 'Do you believe that I am able to do this?'

They said to Him, 'Yes, Lord.' Then He touched their eyes, saying, 'According to your faith let it be to you.'" Matthew 9:27–29 (NKJV)

"Then Jesus went about all the cities and villages, teaching in their synagogues, preaching the gospel of the kingdom, and healing every sickness and every disease among the people." Matthew 9:35 (NKJV)

"And when He had called His twelve disciples to Him, He gave them power over unclean spirits, to cast them out, and to heal all kinds of sickness and all kinds of disease." Matthew 10:1(NKJV)

"And as you go, preach, saying, 'The kingdom of heaven is at hand. Heal the sick, cleanse the lepers, raise the dead, cast out demons. Freely you have received, freely give.'" Matthew 10:7–8 (NKJV)

"And behold, there was a man who had a withered hand. And they asked Him, saying, 'Is it lawful to heal on the Sabbath?'—that they might accuse Him. Then He said to them, 'What man is there among you who has one sheep, and if it falls into a pit on the Sabbath, will not lay hold of it and lift it out? Of how much more value then is a man than a sheep? Therefore it is lawful to do good on the Sabbath.' Then He said to the man, 'Stretch out your hand.' And he stretched it out, and it was restored as whole as the other." Matthew 12:10–13 (NKJV)

"Then the Pharisees went out and plotted against Him, how they might destroy Him. But when Jesus knew it, He withdrew from there. And great multitudes followed Him, and He healed them all." Matthew 12:14–15 (NKJV)

"For the hearts of this people have grown dull. Their ears are hard of hearing, And their eyes they have closed, Lest they should see with their eyes and hear with their ears, Lest they should understand with their hearts and turn, So that I should heal them." Matthew 13:15 (NKJV)

"Then Jesus answered and said to her, 'O woman, great is your faith! Let it be to you as you desire.' And her daughter was healed from that very hour." Matthew 15:28 (NKJV), (also see Mark 7:24–30)

"Then great multitudes came to Him, having with them the lame, blind, mute, maimed, and many others; and they laid them down at Jesus' feet, and He healed them." Matthew 15:30(NKJV), (also see Mark 7:31–37)

"And when they had come to the multitude, a man came to Him, kneeling down to Him and saying, 'Lord, have mercy on my son, for he is an epileptic and suffers severely; for he often falls into the fire and often into the water. So I brought him to Your disciples, but they could not cure him.' Then Jesus answered and said, 'O faithless and perverse generation, how long shall I be with you? How long shall I bear with you? Bring him here to Me.' And Jesus rebuked the demon, and it came out of him; and the child was cured from that very hour." Matthew 17:14–18 (NKJV)

"And great multitudes followed Him, and He healed them there." Matthew 19:2 (NKJV)

"Then the blind and the lame came to Him in the temple, and He healed them." Matthew 21:14 (NKJV)

"Now as soon as they had come out of the synagogue, they entered the house of Simon and Andrew, with James and John. But Simon's wife's mother lay sick with a fever, and they told Him about her at once. So He came and took her by the hand and lifted her up, and immediately the fever left her. And she served them." Mark 1:29–31 (NKJV)

"Now a leper came to Him, imploring Him, kneeling down to Him and saying to Him, 'If You are willing, You can make me clean.' Then Jesus, moved with compassion, stretched out His hand and touched him, and said to him, 'I am willing; be cleansed.'" Mark 1:40–41 (NKJV)

"For He healed many, so that as many as had afflictions pressed about Him to touch Him." Mark 3:10 (NKJV)

"And He went up on the mountain and called to Him those He Himself wanted. And they came to Him. Then He appointed twelve, that they might be with Him and that He might send them out to preach, and to have power to heal sicknesses and to cast out demons." Mark 3:13–15 (NKJV)

"But when He was alone, those around Him with the twelve asked Him about the parable. And He said to them, "To you it has been given to know the mystery of the kingdom of God; but to those who are outside, all things come in parables, so that 'Seeing they may see and not perceive, and hearing they may hear and not understand; Lest they should turn, And their sins be forgiven them.' " Mark 4:10–12 (NKJV)

"And behold, one of the rulers of the synagogue came, Jairus by name. And when he saw Him, he fell at His feet and begged Him earnestly, saying, 'my little daughter lies at the point of death. Come and lay Your hands on her, that she may be healed, and she will live.'" Mark 5:22–23 (NKJV), (also see Matthew 9:18–19, Luke 8:41–42)

"For she said, 'If only I may touch His clothes, I shall be made well.' Immediately the fountain of her blood was dried up, and she felt in her body that she was healed of the affliction." Mark 5:28–29 (NKJV), (also see Matthew 9:20–22, Luke 8:43–48)

"Now He could do no mighty work there, except that He laid His hands on a few sick people and healed them." Mark 6:5 (NKJV)

"And they cast out many demons, and anointed with oil many who were sick, and healed them." Mark 6:13 (NKJV)

"Wherever He entered, into villages, cities, or the country, they laid the sick in the marketplaces, and begged Him that they might just touch the hem of His garment. And as many as touched Him were made well." Mark 6:56 (NKJV)

"Then they brought to Him one who was deaf and had an impediment in his speech, and they begged Him to put His hand on him. And He took him aside from the multitude, and put His fingers in his ears, and He spat and touched his tongue. Then, looking up to heaven, He sighed, and said to him, 'Ephphatha,' that is, 'Be opened.' Immediately his ears were opened, and the impediment of his tongue was loosed, and he spoke plainly." Mark 7:32–35 (NKJV).

"For assuredly, I say to you, whoever says to this mountain, 'Be removed and be cast into the sea,' and does not doubt in his heart, but believes that those things he says will be done, he will have whatever he says. Therefore I say to you, whatever things you ask when you pray, believe that you receive them, and you will have them. And whenever you stand praying, if you have anything against anyone, forgive him, that your Father in heaven may also forgive you your trespasses. But if you do not forgive, neither will your Father in heaven forgive your trespasses." Mark 11:23–26 (NKJV)

"And many lepers were in Israel in the time of Elisha the prophet, and none of them was cleansed except Naaman the Syrian." Luke 4:27 (NKJV)

"However, the report went around concerning Him all the more; and great multitudes came together to hear, and to be healed by Him of their infirmities." Luke 5:15 (NKJV)

"And He came down with them and stood on a level place with a crowd of His disciples and a great multitude of people from all Judea and Jerusalem, and from the seacoast of Tyre and Sidon, who came to hear Him and be healed of their diseases, as well as those who were tormented with unclean spirits. And they were healed. And the whole multitude sought to touch Him, for power went out from Him and healed them all." Luke 6:17–19 (NKJV)

"They also who had seen it told them by what means he who had been demon-possessed was healed." Luke 8:36 (NKJV)

"Now a woman, having a flow of blood for twelve years, who had spent all her livelihood on physicians and could not be healed by any, came from behind and touched the border of His garment. And immediately her flow of blood stopped." Luke 8:43–44 (NKJV), (also see Matthew 9:20–22, Mark 5:21–34).

"'And whoever will not receive you, when you go out of that city, shake off the very dust from your feet as a testimony against them.' So they departed and went through the towns, preaching the gospel and healing everywhere." Luke 9:5–6 (NKJV)

"But when the multitudes knew it, they followed Him; and He received them and spoke to them about the kingdom of God, and healed those who had need of healing." Luke 9:11 (NKJV)

"Then Jesus answered and said, 'O faithless and perverse generation, how long shall I be with you and bear with you? Bring your son here.' And as he was still coming, the demon threw him down and convulsed him. Then Jesus rebuked the unclean spirit, healed the child, and gave him back to his father." Luke 9:41–42 (NKJV), (also see Matthew 17:14–18, Mark 9:14–27)

"Now He was teaching in one of the synagogues on the Sabbath. And behold, there was a woman who had a spirit of infirmity eighteen years, and was bent over and could in no way raise herself up. But when Jesus saw her, He called her to Him and said to her, 'Woman, you are loosed from your infirmity.' And He laid His hands on her, and immediately she was made straight, and glorified God." Luke 13:11–13 (NKJV)

"And one of them, when he saw that he was healed, returned, and with a loud voice glorified God, and fell down on his face at His feet, giving Him thanks. And he was a Samaritan." Luke 17:15–16 (NKJV)

"And one of them struck the servant of the high priest and cut off his right ear. But Jesus answered and said, 'Permit even this.' And He touched his ear and healed him." Luke 22:50–51 (NKJV)

"But the one who was healed did not know who it was, for Jesus had withdrawn, a multitude being in that place." John 5:13 (NKJV)

"When Jesus heard *that*, He said, "This sickness is not unto death, but for the glory of God, that the Son of God may be glorified through it." John 11:4 (NKJV)

"He has blinded their eyes and hardened their hearts, Lest they should see with their eyes, Lest they should understand with their hearts and turn, So that I should heal them." John 12:40 (NKJV)

"Then Peter said, 'Silver and gold I do not have, but what I do have I give you: In the name of Jesus Christ of Nazareth, rise up and walk.'" Acts 3:6 (NKJV)

"For the man was over forty years old on whom this miracle of healing had been performed." Acts 4:22 (NKJV)

"Now, Lord, look on their threats, and grant to Your servants that with all boldness they may speak Your word, by stretching out Your hand to heal, and that signs and wonders may be done through the name of Your holy Servant Jesus." Acts 4:29–30 (NKJV)

"Also a multitude gathered from the surrounding cities to Jerusalem, bringing sick people and those who were tormented by unclean spirits, and they were all healed." Acts 5:16 (NKJV)

"And the multitudes with one accord heeded the things spoken by Philip, hearing and seeing the miracles which he did. For unclean spirits, crying with a loud voice, came out of many who were possessed; and many who were paralyzed and lame were healed. And there was great joy in that city." Acts 8:6–8 (NKJV)

"And Peter said to him, 'Aeneas, Jesus the Christ heals you. Arise and make your bed.' Then he arose immediately." Acts 9:34 (NKJV)

"The word which God sent to the children of Israel, preaching peace through Jesus Christ—He is Lord of all—that word you know, which was proclaimed throughout all Judea, and began from Galilee after the baptism which John preached: how God anointed Jesus of Nazareth with the Holy Spirit and with power, who went about doing good and healing all who were oppressed by the devil, for God was with Him." Acts 10:36–39 (NKJV)

"And in Lystra a certain man without strength in his feet was sitting, a cripple from his mother's womb, who had never walked. This man heard Paul speaking. Paul, observing him intently and seeing that he had faith to be healed, said with a loud voice, 'Stand up straight on your feet!' And he leaped and walked." Acts 14:8–10 (NKJV)

"And it happened that the father of Publius lay sick of a fever and dysentery. Paul went in to him and prayed, and he laid his hands on him and healed him. So when this was done, the rest of those on the island who had diseases also came and were healed." Acts 28:8–9 (NKJV)

"Having then gifts differing according to the grace that is given to us, let us use them: if prophecy, let us prophesy in proportion to our faith; or ministry, let us use it in our ministering; he who teaches, in teaching; he who exhorts, in exhortation; he who gives, with liberality; he who leads, with diligence; he who shows mercy, with cheerfulness." Romans 12:6–8 (NKJV)

"But the natural man does not receive the things of the Spirit of God, for they are foolishness to him; nor can he know them, because they are spiritually discerned." 1 Corinthians 2:14 (NKJV)

"But the manifestation of the Spirit is given to each one for the profit of all: for to one is given the word of wisdom through the Spirit, to another the word of knowledge through the same Spirit, to another faith by the same Spirit, to another gifts of healings by the same Spirit, to another the working of miracles, to another prophecy, to another discerning of spirits, to another different kinds of tongues, to another the interpretation of tongues. But one and the same Spirit works all these things, distributing to each one individually as He wills. For as the body is one and has many members, but all the members of that one body, being many, are one body, so also is Christ." 1 Corinthians 12:7–12 (NKJV)

"And He Himself gave some to be apostles, some prophets, some evangelists, and some pastors and teachers, for the equipping of the saints for the work of ministry, for the edifying of the body of Christ, till we all come to the unity of the faith and of the knowledge of the Son of God, to a perfect man, to the measure of the stature of the fullness of Christ." Ephesians 4:11–13 (NKJV)

"Therefore strengthen the hands which hang down, and the feeble knees, and make straight paths for your feet, so that what is lame may not be dislocated, but rather be healed." Hebrews 12:12–13 (NKJV)

"Who Himself bore our sins in His own body on the tree, that we, having died to sins, might live for righteousness—by whose stripes you were healed." 1 Peter 2:24 (NKJV)

"Confess your trespasses to one another, and pray for one another, that you may be healed. The effective, fervent prayer of a righteous man avails much." James 5:16 (NKJV)

"And he showed me a pure river of water of life, clear as crystal, proceeding from the throne of God and of the Lamb. In the middle of its street, and on either side of the river, was the tree of life, which bore twelve fruits, each tree yielding its fruit every month. The leaves of the tree were for the healing of the nations." Revelation 22:1–2 (NKJV)

Notes

1. Gal. 3:13
2. Acts 2:28; Hebrews 10:18
3. Romans 3:23, 5:8, 6:23
4. We Are Church, objects to JPII canonization. (September 30, 2013). Retrieved October 2, 2013, from http://ncron line.org/blogs/we-are-church-objects-jpii-canonization
5. Jamieson, R., Fausset, A. R., & Brown, D. (1997). *Commentary Critical and Explanatory on the Whole Bible* (Lk 4:24). Oak Harbor, WA: Logos Research Systems, Inc.